Miniat

Miniature Cows as pets

Miniature Cows Keeping, Pros and Cons, Care,
Housing, Diet and Health all included

by

Roger Rodendale

Table of Contents

Introduction

Cows are fuzzy and gentle beings that make wonderful and practical pets. When you think of the simple farm life, you think of a fenced area that contains a few cows tethered there. The best part about cows is that they thrive on the simple things such as cut and carry forage or any root crop from your garden. The fact that they are gentle makes it possible for you to have children and cows in the same family.

Cut to the urban life that we lead today, a large sized cow is certainly not an option thanks to all the space constraints. In addition to this, you have several regulations that govern the size of the animal that you can have in your home.

If you dream of having a family cow in your home, you can definitely opt for a miniature cow if you can fulfill all the requirements for your cow. In fact, several hobby farmers rally for miniature cattle as they are convenient, easy to manage and are perfectly sized for our urban set up.

All miniature cow owners unanimously agree that they are great pets. In fact, they are often compared to a large dog with additional benefits like having access to fresh milk! Even for owners who have brought home adult cows, the experience has been nothing but positive. They are able to form great bonds with their miniature cows.

These creatures are quiet natured and are extremely friendly. They are even useful to perform tasks within your farm or yard such as carrying tools. These bovines are extremely intelligent and can be trained to be a great companion.

The good thing about miniature cows is that they are not as intimidating as the full sized ones. They also have personalities that are quite engaging, making them more approachable.

While the miniature cow seems like a perfectly good pet to bring home, you need to be aware of the right care and requirements to keep the animal healthy. From managing a hygienic ambience to keeping your cow well fed and well exercised, all the functions to keep the cow in good health are your prerogative.

With this book, you will be able to understand all the basics of bringing the miniature cow home, making sure that you give them the right environment to stay safe in and also providing them with proper food and healthcare.

The book is written as a guide to those who already have a miniature cow as well as those who are considering bringing one home as a pet. The information is exhaustive and is the result of several insights from previous miniature cow owners.

Summing up, this book consists of practical tips that will help you solve any issue that you may be facing with your pet. It is also a treasure trove of all the information you need to know if you are truly ready for a miniature cow and to prepare you for your bovine companion.

Chapter 1: What is a Miniature Cow?

For most people the concept of a miniature cow or miniature cattle itself may seem quite laughable. It is almost as if they aren't the real deal.

Usually, the first question that comes up is why anyone would want a miniature cow. And, the second concern is if these are regular sized cows with some genetic or developmental defects. To learn more about these two common queries we will have to take a peek into the history of cattle and their association with people.

1. History of downsizing

Modern cattle can be traced back to almost six thousand years using the archaeological evidences. Two species, namely the *Bos taurus or the* hump-less cattle or the *Bos indicus or the* humped cattle are believed to be the predecessors of the modern domesticated cattle. These two species were generated by another species which is classified as *Bos primigenius.*

It has been noticed that these cattle gradually reduced in size because of inadequate feeding. It is also believed that they were downsized deliberately to be able to handle them and house them properly. The recent findings revealed several remains of cattle that were not only less bulky but also smaller in size.

Around the 19th century, certain breeds that hailed from the British Iles such as the Jerseys, Dexters and Kerrys were prized for their small stature and were chosen as decorations in county estates. They also gained popularity because of their ability to mow the lawns naturally.

In Northern Europe, it was a norm to have a family cow or a small-sized herd. They were raised to provide milk and meat and also to help in cultivation.

In the tropical regions, a family cow is still a common occurrence with preference given to the smaller breeds such as the Zebu cattle.

Current statistics reveal that a cow in the United States, on an average, weighs about 1300 pounds. Records show that less than 60 years ago, cows did not weigh more than 900 pounds.

Post Second World War, demand for better quality meat increased. In addition to that, resources for better nutrition, breeding and feeding also became available. With an increase in production capabilities, the mindset shifted towards " the bigger the better".

This move was supported by producers as it would increase their profits tremendously. Cattle that had longer legs and more height were easier to herd as they would lose less weight and feel less stressed even when moved across large rangelands. As for the dairymen, with larger cows, milk production would increase, as the larger calves that were the result of this would need more food.

With these developments and with better facilities of transport and refrigeration, larger cows began to gain popularity. While the whole world was shifting towards large sized cattle, there were some who were still researching about the smaller breeds and methods to produce healthy specimens of these breeds.

In the late 1960s, breeding of smaller zebu cattle was started by a Mexican rancher. He admitted that he wanted to create miniature cattle as a pet for those who could afford it. He then partnered with a veterinary researcher and shifted the focus of the project towards producing more on a smaller piece of land. This drew the interest of several organizations across the world, the most noteworthy one being the US National Research Council.

Then, a Texas breeder noticed that the size of the cows and cattle on the show ring was steadily on the rise. So, he decided to start a program to downsize the Hereford Cattle in the 1970s. This breed hails from Herefordshire in England. The goal of this breeder was to produce specimens that were smaller in size but excellent in their conformation.

Simultaneously, a research project was being conducted in Australia. This project that went on from 1974 to 1993 was primarily focused on determining if the smaller specimens of Angus cattle were more efficient in producing meat. This led to the production of the Lowline breed. This breed was used as the closed herd of small sized cattle in this project. The efficiency was the same as the larger cows and thus, the interest in this breed continued, allowing them to survive.

In Seattle, Washington, around the same time, breeders Arlene Gradwohl and Richard Gradwohl noticed that urbanization was happening quickly. There were several housing developments that began to mushroom around the area. Being a farm man himself, Richard wanted to make sure that he was able to retain the rural lifestyle. He had a background as a business professor and he began to research about the commercial value of the possible opportunities to maintain a farm life.

He realized that smaller cattle had greater value on smaller property. Since he advocated innovation, he began his research on miniature cattle and acquired livestock and learnt line-breeding techniques. Then he got extremely interested in developing new breeds of these miniature cows. He has developed almost 18 new breeds of miniature cattle.

It is true that the third world countries and other developing nations still maintain interest in the larger breeds. But several farm owners have realized that it is futile to pursue larger cattle. In fact, during the 1980's research conducted by the National Research Council helped raise awareness in almost 80 countries about the potential of miniature cattle. This, they claimed, would actually help develop these nations.

In the United States, there have been significant changes in farming. The amount of land available has reduced and several hobby farms and small acreages have gained popularity. A census of agriculture in 2002 revealed that there has been an increase in small farms by 46% since 1979. There have also been several changes in farm ownerships giving rise to new typology groups such as retirement farms and lifestyle farms. Today, most farm operators are the sole owners as well.

There are tax incentives for small scale farmers. They can get benefits by showing any use of land for agricultural purposes. For many, farming is a way of life post retirement, some own small farms for ecological reasons, natural living reasons and also the desire to lead a simple farm life. This is one of the significant reasons for growing interest in Miniature cattle.

The most important thing for anyone who is interested in miniature cattle to know is that these are not dwarfed versions of larger cattle. They are new breeds that just tend to look smaller in proportions. Dwarfism does occur among miniature cows such as the Bulldog syndrome in the Dexter breed. These issues are severe genetic problems. However, miniature cattle are not large cattle with genetic conditions.

2. Size standards for miniature cows

There are a few guidelines for recognizing miniature cattle. These size standards have been put in place to help you bring home a healthy pet. The international Miniature Cattle Breeders Society and Registry was founded in 1989 by the Gradwohls and it follows these measurements:

- 42 inches at the hip in case of a 3 year old cattle as the full height.

- The weight as this age must vary between 500 and 700 pounds.

- Up to 48 inches is considered a mid-sized immature cattle.

A registry with these measurements was maintained by the Gradwohls for 28 breeds of miniature cattle.

A new breed called "microcattle: was reported by the National Research Council. These breeds measured at 300 kilos or less without any restriction in terms of height. According to the Gradwohls, any specimen shorter than 36 inches can be categorized as microcattle.

There are a few breeds that have specific guidelines. You can find official clubs dedicated to each of these breeds, such as the Miniature Hereford Breeders Association, who have websites that list all necessary characteristics. The assigned standards for a few breeds are:

- Dexter cattle: Bulls measure between 38-44 inches and weigh less than 1000 pounds. Cows measure between 36 to 42 inches and weigh less than 750 pounds.

- Hereford cattle: Bulls measure a maximum height of 48 inches while cows measure a maximum of 45 inches.

- Miniature Zebu cattle: The bulls and cows cannot exceed more than 42 inches when measured at the withers. Bulls weigh between 400 to 600 pounds and cows measure between 300-500 pounds.

These standards show us that miniature cattle start off really small. Calves measure 19 to 22 inches which is almost the same as the length of human babies. Some of them may be about 30 inches. The weight of the cattle is not more than 65 pounds and this varies from one breed to another.

The standards are an average measurement to determine if a specimen is healthy or not. If you are solely into hobby breeding and farming, a few inches of deviation from standards will not matter. However, in case of miniature cattle shows, it is imperative to stick to the standards that have been established for specific breeds in order to qualify to showcase your cattle.

3. Breeds of miniature cattle

As mentioned before, several breeds of miniature cattle have been developed over the years. Each breed has its own utilitarian value and there are reasons why some people prefer a certain breed. The major breeds in the United States are:

Dexters

- The authorities on the standardization of this breed are the American Dexter Cattle Association and the Purebred Dexter Cattle Association of North America.

- These breeds were bred to be the original small area cattle from Ireland. They serve a dual purpose.

- These cattle have always been smaller in size which has made them popular in breeding programs in order to create smaller varieties of other breeds.

- These animals are known for their gentle nature. They are extremely fertile and provide a good quantity of milk.

- Over 600 farmers and producers have been listed by the Purebred Dexter Cattle Association of North America. Over 50 states are involved actively in the production of this species.

- There are three colors of Dexters including red, dun and black.

- Most of these animals are horned but some polled Dexters have been introduced recently. In an interview given in 2007, Richard Gradwohl said that he is currently developing White Dexters.

Miniature Herefords

- The authorities on standardization of this breed are The Miniature Hereford Breeders Association and the Miniature Hereford Clun. You can register your cow or bull with the American Hereford Association.

- These miniatures are red in color with white faces just like the full sized ones. They may have horns or may be polled.

- They were included in the National Western Stock show for the first time in the year 2000.

- A steady increase in numbers was noticed not just in the United States but in Canada as well.

- Among nineteen breeds that were entered in a recent show, this breed ranked tenth.

- They have also been included in the International Livestock Exposition since November 2007.

- It is estimated that the count of Miniature Herefords has increased to 3000 and they are found in almost 40 states in the US alone.

Lowlines

- The authorities for the standardization of this breed are the American Lowline Registry.

- They are basically a smaller version of Angus cattle.

- In the United States, they have become extremely popular and have the same status as companies like John Deere Green in terms of beef production.

- Although they were introduced only in 1996, they have gained a lot of popularity.

- Today you will find these animals in all the states in the USA except for seven.

Jerseys

- The authorities for standardization are the American Miniature Jersey Registry and Association.

- They are the most widely spread miniature dairy breed in the United States.

- Besides the fact that they are great milk producers, this breed has become popular for their sheer cuteness with coloring that is deer like.

- There are 21 member states in the Jersey registry.

- This breed is also a popular choice for breeding programs that create smaller versions of cattle breed because of their already small stature.

Other breeds

There are many miniature cattle breeds that are being developed on a regular basis with a lot of support from enthusiasts. They are lower in numbers but have had a lot of mention in research and also in cattle shows.

One such breed is the Miniature Zebu that is supported by the Miniature Zebu Association. This breed is known for being extremely resistant to heat and diseases.

This is a humped miniature breed that has been bred for the appearance. As per the information, this is the smallest miniature breed that has been developed. There are about 30 states that list members of this breed.

There is also a registry of cattle that lists miniature varieties of Shorthorn cattle. They are preferred for the beef and dairy production abilities. They are either polled or horned.

In the 1920s, one breed called the Texas longhorn almost became extinct. They received an appropriation from the Congress that allowed the Texas Longhorn Breeders Association to create new specimens in about 40 states.

This breed is known for its unique colors and markings. They have distinctive horns that are almost square which means that the horns are almost exact in size when measured from tip to tip.

Another popular miniature breed is the Miniature Highland. These long haired cows and bulls are known for their distinct appearance. Although there are no exact records of how diverse the range of this breed is, they have become quite popular and have been likened to Ewoks from Star Wars! The hardiness, the grazing brush and the thick hide of this breed is the reason for their popularity.

One of the most popular breeds in Australia is the Miniature Galloway, which has a double hair coat. These animals are usually listed as mid-sized because of the established standards that state that the specimens are less than 50 pounds in weight and 42 inches in height when they are about 11 months old.

This breed is normally used for cross breeding and for the production of new breeds of miniature cattle. They come in a range of colors including red, dun, black and white.

Today, the International Miniature Cattle Breeders Society lists about 28 species of miniature breeds. Because of constant work from breeders like the Gradwohls, there are new ones that are growing in different areas.

You can visit the website of the IMCBS for more information on the right methods of producing miniature breeds to earn a good profit. There are also details on trademarking a new breed developed by you.

There are several reasons why new breeds are developed. Some of them want specific physical traits to create smaller varieties for the pet market in general. The IMCBS also tells you in detail how the registered breeds were developed so you can get an idea. The possibilities are limitless as long as breeders are genuine and work under the guidelines provided to make sure that the cattle produced is healthy and utilitarian.

4. Why choose miniature cattle?

The best thing about miniature cattle is that they have the same qualities as their large sized counterparts. They are also more convenient to manage in an urban set up. That is why several farm owners are switching to miniature cattle. Some of the best reasons to own miniature cattle are:

They don't need much space

In case of full sized cattle, you need five acres for two head. In case of miniature cattle, you can have two per acre of land. This depends on the grass available and the supplements that you provide with the feed.

Cattle do well when raised in herds. It is possible to have one or more herds even on a smaller property when you raise miniature cattle.

Gentler personality

In comparison to their large sized counterparts, miniature cattle tend to be more docile. Since they are small in size and easy to manage, their owners work directly with them from birth. That makes it possible to halter train them at a very young age. It is also much easier to control miniature cattle should they get out of hand.

The fact that they are easier to handle makes them a better choice for women and also to those who have retired. With large cattle, it can be a little intimidating, especially if you have kids at home.

Lower maintenance costs

The costs per head are very low in case of miniature cattle. It is possible even to use regular cattle equipment and it will last longer with miniature cattle. Even the cost of housing and confinement is really low. You do not have to make fencing too tall which means that it is cheaper.

Return on investment

Miniature cattle can be pricey. In order to get started, you will have to make a big investment. The price can vary and can be over $1000 or £500 per head. It depends on the rarity of the breed, the availability and the breeding heritage.

In some cases, breeds that have been developed with specific traits and qualities can cost tens of thousands of dollars. But, when you enter your cattle into breeding programs, you may be able to create more than one specimen of your breed or may be lucky enough to develop new species altogether. Either way, you will be able to get guaranteed returns on your investments with miniature cattle.

Varied uses

One of the most important reasons for the increased popularity of smaller cattle is their value on farms and in commercial purposes. They have in fact proved to be a lot more efficient in terms of dairy production, beef production, breeding and also as show cattle.

Of course, they also make great pets besides being very useful commercially. They have a very friendly nature that also makes them perfect for petting zoos and to educate more people through agro-tourism.

Selling miniature cattle or using them for the same can be good business. The population of miniatures is still low in comparison to the regular sized ones but the demand increases by almost 20% per annum.

There are requirements that include a good record about the heritage if the cattle, documentation of their size when they are born, the immunization records and also the ease of calving. You can sell the breeding samples of your miniature cattle for a good price. Per straw of breeding sample can earn you between $50-100 or £10-50. You can sell embryos for as high as $1500 or £700.

Of course beef production is an important use. Today healthy and hormone free meat is in demand and that makes miniature cattle a good option for farm owners. Dairy production is, of course, one of the biggest income generators for farm owners. There are certain breeds like the Dexters that provide both and have, therefore, become popular.

You do not have to worry about quantity either. With breeds like miniature Jerseys, you can get almost 4 gallons of milk each day with no compromise on the butterfat content and the protein content. If you are raising miniature cattle as pets, this can become a source of fresh milk for your family.

Miniature breeds are eligible for several national and state level cattle shows which have attractive cash prizes. The sheer interest in miniature cattle and the curiosity about them has become a USP, promoting their use in cattle shows. The respective clubs for miniature cattle have also started special shows in various categories such as pre- junior categories for younger bulls and cows.

Of course, they are increasingly becoming popular as house pets. While this is still a new practice, several farms and breeders have reported an increase in sales solely to keep miniature cattle as pets. Keeping a miniature cow as a pet comes with several benefits. Aside from the fact that they make great companions, they are also great lawn mowers and produce a good amount of manure.

There are a few concerns with miniature cattle making their way into the urban set up. One of them is space. You need to have ample space for the cattle to graze. Fenced areas with adequate housing is very important. You also need to have good back up when you need to travel. It is, after all, not as simple as getting your neighbor or friend to take care of your pet dog or cat.

We will deal with these concerns in the following chapters. The thing with miniature cows and bulls is that they are cheaper than full sized counterparts but do require good funding in order to raise healthy pets. Only when you are prepared to take good care of them and have the resources to do so should you buy miniature cattle for your home.

Once you have a miniature cow or bull, they can perform small tasks like drawing carts, mowing your lawn or even coming handy in your child's 4-H programs. Of course, they make very loving and gentle pets.

Chapter 2: Preparing for Your Miniature Cow

There are a few considerations that you need to make before you bring a miniature cow home:

- You need to have a large enough space for each member of your herd.

- You must have enough finances to provide good quality food and healthcare for your pets.

- They need to have a place to take shelter and rest.

- You need to be aware of the right way to interact with your miniature cows to stay safe and to make sure that they animals are not stressed.

There are a few things that you have to keep prepared before you bring your miniature cow home.

1. Where to buy a miniature cow

The first step is to figure out the best source for your miniature cow. The most common options include:

- A breeder: There are commercial and hobby breeders who work towards producing a single breed of mini cattle or try to experiment with different breeds and genetic lines. You need to make sure that the breeder that you are planning to buy from has positive testimonies, maintains a clean and hygienic environment for his cows and bulls and has ample knowledge about minis.

- A primary owner: Sometimes, owners may be interested in selling or giving away calves that were born in their yard or farm. These individuals are not breeders and are probably the best source as they do not have any agenda with their calves. These people are genuinely concerned about the health and safety of the herd.

- Auctions: in case of rare breeds, there may be auctions at state shows and fairs. This is risky as you do not know what health or behavioral issues the cow or bull may have. Buying from an auction is generally not recommended for first time buyers.

- Rescue/ shelter: This is the most economical option available to you. However, the breed may be poor in quality and may come with several health issues as well.

Buying options with mini cows

When you buy your miniature cow, make sure that you choose the breed according to the purpose that it will serve on your farm. We have discussed the qualities of different breeds in the previous chapter. Since they are extremely expensive, learning all you can about your preferred breed will help you choose a healthy specimen.

Always make sure that you buy from reputable breeder. Secondly, you must insist on a health check up by a vet before you bring one home.

If you want to get started with your miniature herd right away, you can choose purebred adults and breeding stock. They are the most expensive option and are also not easily available in most cases. You can consider buying calves because they are more readily available. The disadvantage with calves is that they do not come with a breeding guarantee. So if the calf grows up to be poor in production, you will lose out on your investment. A calf is a good option if you are not particularly interested in breeding and are looking for a low price option.

For some breeds, it is also possible to purchase the embryos. But you can do so only if you have the knowledge and facilities or necessary assistance for successful embryo transfers in your cattle.

You have the option of buying frozen embryos or one that has been implanted in a female already. The latter is the cheaper and safer option. In case of embryo implantation, the success rate varies. It is usually about 60% on an average.

In case you decide to purchase frozen embryos, you must consider meeting a reproductive specialist who deals with cattle solely. Make sure you gain as much knowledge as possible. It is also important to choose a healthy cow for implantation. Ones that are easy calvers are preferred to improve success rates. If you are looking at a regular sized cow, make sure that the height is small enough for a new born mini cow to reach the udder and suckle.

There are many risks with purchasing embryos. The success rate is not 100% to begin with. You also cannot determine the gender of the calf that will be born. Only when you are looking for an extremely rare breed, you may not have too many other options to pursue.

Adopting a miniature cow

Some farms will put their calves up for adoption. You may also adopt one from a rescue shelter. In case of the latter option, be prepared for possible behavioral issues in the cow as they may have had a history of abuse or poor treatment.

Now, with adoption, you only have to pay an adoption fee for your cow or calf. This starts as low as $30 or £12 depending upon the medical history of the animal and the expenses borne for the animal.

The cows, bulls or calves up for adoption will be listed on the website of the shelter or farm that you plan to adopt from. You can look for one with all the desirable traits. Make sure that you visit the animal that you have chosen at least once to ensure that the temperament suits your home. You need to be particularly careful when you are adopting a bull as you need to be cautious when you are approaching them, especially when the breeding season is on.

Once you have transferred the adoption fee, you will have to send in all your personal details. They may require a few documents of identity as well. Then, the miniature cattle that you have selected will either be delivered to your home or you may have to pick him up, depending upon the conditions of the place you are adopting from. Some of them insist on house checks as well. Once the adoption process is complete, it is good to get your pet checked by a vet immediately. In some cases, you will be able to get a health guarantee that allows you to return the animal you adopted, provided he has been checked in less than 72 hours of delivery.

Choosing the best breed

Once you have found a good breeder whom you can buy a good miniature cattle breed from, the next step is to decide which one suits you best. Each breed has a different requirement and temperament that you need to cater to.

The origin of the breed is the first thing that you must consider. The next thing is to understand the breeds that your mini is a mixture of. This will help broadly determine the characteristics of the breed and the type of environment that you will need to provide.

Your interest in bringing a miniature cow is also important. The resources available and the type of care that you will be able to provide will also determine which breed you must choose as a pet.

Now, if you are just looking for a family cow, a dual purpose breed like the Dexter is the best option. They will be able to provide your family with milk on a daily basis. On the other hand, if you are looking for a herd, you need to consider factors like the local climate, the weather pattern, the type of pasture that you have and the space available. Some breeds are adaptable to cold climate, specifically the double coated ones and others will do well in hot climate.

The nature of the cow that you bring home matters if you want a family cow. One that is easier to handle, with a gentle disposition, is the best option for you. Miniature Herefords are known for being extremely gentle and mellow. They are best when you have children in your home. That said, remember that there are animals that have a good or poor disposition in every breed. So, make sure that you spend some time with the one that you have chosen before you make the final decision.

Try to learn as much as you can about the breed that you have set your mind on. The more you learn, the more you will be able to look into the details of their behavior. For example, angus cattle are known for their marbling ability while Herefords are known for being placid in nature and also for their high feed efficiency.

Some breeds are known for being very high yielding in milk. But, if it costs more to feed them, you may not have too many profits. It is best that you find a hardier breed that will be able to function even with marginal pastures if you are looking at a commercial venture. If they are good at calving, you will also see that the cow will stay longer with the herd, providing more milk.

In the end, the only thing that determines what breed that you choose is the purpose of bringing one home. Some are specifically chosen as companions, some make great show animals and some are commercially more viable.

It is recommended that you choose local breeds as they are likely to adapt faster. They will be able to handle the weather fluctuations and will be healthier. However, with the right resources, you can raise a healthy herd of any breed. As long as you are willing to learn more and provide for your pet, you can choose any breed for your home. But, do not make a choice because you have a favorite when you also know that it will be a challenge to provide for him or her.

2. Shelter for the herd

There are different ways of keeping a herd. You can either have an extensive area for grazing or can keep the herd in close confinement. But, it is your responsibility to make sure that you provide for the welfare of your herd. The basic needs are food, fresh air, clean water and shelter. In fact, not providing ample shelter from extreme weather conditions amounts to animal cruelty in many states.

A healthy herd can tolerate weather changes to a large extent provided they have good access to fresh water and food and have been acclimatized. In any case, providing shelter will ensure that no production ability is lost. When the herd does not have enough shelter, a lot of their energy goes into just taking care of normal functions.

If the temperature goes above or below the average temperature that the animal can handle, you have to make sure that you provide them with adequate shelter. It is possible for deaths to occur in your herd because of extreme weather conditions.

Dealing with adverse weather
Any extremities including temperature dropping suddenly or increasing suddenly can be categorized as adverse weather. This includes wind and rain, sudden drop in temperatures or heat waves. Miniature cattle have ways of dealing with this naturally but when the temperatures are too extreme, they need adequate shelter.

Coping with heat
Respiration is the primary method of heat loss in cattle. They also transfer the heat into the air and cool off when sweat evaporates. You need to provide shelter that will protect the animals from direct sun. That way the heat load reduces by almost 50%. This ensures that your cattle does not have any exhaustion due to heat stress.

Pregnant cattle and calves are at the highest risk of dying due to a heat shock. This is because they have lower heat resistance. This is also true with any cattle that may have respiratory diseases.

When shade is available, you will see that cattle will rest during the warmer parts of the day and will only graze as the day gets cooler.

If your farm or yard does not have any trees, they will spend time near any water source and will only feed at night. Research shows that shade is preferred over water because that allows the cattle to spend more time resting.

The animals that are at risk of heat related stress are:

- Young animals
- Animals with darker fur

- Dairy cows that produce a high amount of milk
- Animals with poor health
- Obese stock

The best shelter options in hot weather conditions

If you live in a part of the world that tends to have warmer weather, you can choose the following options:

- Shadebelts- This includes a line of deciduous trees that are planted in the east- west direction. That provides shade on the southern part. You can prune the trees regularly to help improve air circulation.

- Constructed shelters that usually include wooden or iron poles with a roof of shade cloth, timber or iron.

- You can even plant trees that have large canopies. These trees will give the area a cooling effect thanks to the absorption of heat by the leaves.

Make sure that your cattle has enough water to drink during the warmer months. As a rule miniature cattle will consume close to 100 liters of water when they are producing milk. This will increase when the temperature increases to above 335 degrees C.

Keep the water source close to the shelter so that the cattle can get familiar with it. The volume of the water container should be high enough to cope with demanding conditions. If you have a mixed barn, you have to increase the number of watering points and also improve the water quantity as the temperature increases.

Coping with cold weather

Just like hot weather, cold weather also causes a lot of stress. Cold weather accompanied by rain will reduce the body temperature of the animal. This leads to a drop in weight and also increases the fat content in milk. Cattle that are at high risk of cold related stress are:

- New born calves or pregnant cows
- Sick animals
- Animals that have a low body condition

In these animals cold can also lead to death if it is too extreme. During cold weather, there is an increase in appetite as the animals will need more energy in order to maintain normal body temperature. This means that the food that you provide should be highly digestible. It also helps to increase quantity of food that your miniature cattle finds more palatable. Of course, good shelter helps reduce cold stress effectively.

The best shelter options in hot weather conditions
The shelter that you provide must be able to protect the animals from cold breeze. Some of the best options are:

- Shelters with wind breaks. You will see that the cattle will rub up against the wind break to stay strong. So, you need to make sure that the wind break should be strong and safe.

- If you have a shelterbelt of trees, it will be able to keep the cattle safe from winds. There is a shelter zone that is usually up to about 14 times the height of the shelterbelt.

- Make sure that there are trees in the north-south direction as most wind flow will be in the north and south western direction.

- Paddocks and gullies make good shelter against cold.

When you plant a shelter belt, make sure that the trees are spaced out evenly. That ensures wind flow without too much turbulence.

You must not allow any pregnant cattle to graze in paddocks that have Yellow or Monterey pine trees. If the fallen branches and twigs are ingested, it poses great threat to the fetus.

You can build one sided sheds for your cattle. Temporary shelter can be built using plastic tarpaulins and shade cloth if you do not have any other shelter option.

Shelter is one of the most important parts of proper husbandry of miniature cattle

Building housing areas
Shelterbelts cannot be created overnight. It may take several months for the shelterbelt to grow properly. In case you do not have trees to protect your miniature cattle during adverse weather conditions, here are a few housing options that you can try:

- **Single slope, open sided sheds:** This is the most typical housing option. It is suitable for any livestock that you have on your farm. It is easy to build and is also economical. When you build an open sided shelter, make sure that the open end faces south in the winter to block any wind.

You also have the option of partitioning the pole barns to make sure that the animals are kept at a distance easily.

- **Clear span open sided shelter:** When you have a clear span, you have ample space to use manure removal equipment. You can open any side of this shelter as per the weather. You have a gable end that should be open when there is any rain or snow. With the gable end open, you have more depth in the bay area, protecting the animal from winds.

  The back end of this shelter may become damp and will require ventilation and lighting. This is perfect if you have a herd that is smaller than 20 in number.

- **An unused dairy barn:** This structure can be built but it is a better option if you already have one on your farm. You can renovate it as per the requirement of your miniature cattle. This is cheaper than installing a whole new structure. Make sure you have ample access to manure removal. That is why it is recommended that you have a free stall barn instead of a conventional tie stall.

- **Hoop barn:** This is possibly the most expensive type of shelter for your cattle. But it does provide a lot of protection in cold conditions. However, in the warmer months, ventilation can be a problem. If you have ample grazing space for your cattle, this is not really a big concern. A hoop barn looks almost like a green house with a roof that is arched.

When you are constructing a shelter or housing area for your cattle, here are a few things that you must consider:

- Make sure that the design is simple and practical to maintain it well.

- You must have enough space to make a feed yard to keep the animals comfortable and socialize properly.

- The flooring should be covered with some substrate that can absorb waste. The best option is hay. Mud is not a good idea, especially in winter. Evaporation is lower with mud and if the draining is improper, it can become a harbor for several microbes. If the floor is already made of mud, adding bedding like hay can be a good option.

- The selected area for housing should be higher than the rest of the land. That will help you get rainwater and waste out easily.

- There should be ample light and air supply in the shelter. Sunlight is extremely necessary to keep the shelter dry and prevent any germs or virus from breeding.

- Try to build a shelter in an area that is surrounded by trees. This helps provide additional shade and shelter to the animals.

- There should be a good drainage system inside the shelter to make sure that there is no dampness whatsoever. Trash and excreta in the shelter will lead to the growth of viruses, parasites and insects like mosquitos and flies. They transmit diseases that can affect the entire herd in some cases.

- The shelter should be covered with some form of fencing. We will discuss the options in the next section.

- Make sure that every animal has at least five square meters of space inside the housing area in order to prevent overcrowding and related stress.

- It is a good idea to create a separate area of housing to keep any injured or sick animals in. This should be a quiet and dry area to prevent any stress.

You must have the shelter ready before you bring your miniature cow home. Make sure that it suits the requirements based on the number of cattle and even the age and gender. Younger cattle and bulls will need a shelter that is stronger as they tend to have more energy which means that they are able to apply more force on the walls.

3. Best fencing options
Proper fencing is necessary in order to keep your cattle from entering any unsafe area on your property or from walking out onto a busy street. It also ensures that your cattle are safe from any predators.

You also need good fencing to manage grazing. You can control the area that your cattle grazes in so that they only get access to good fodder. This can be done with the help of temporary fencing. Permanent fences are usually used to mark the boundaries of your property.

Whether you are choosing temporary or permanent fencing, here are the options available:

- **Barbed wire fence:** This type of fence consists of several strands of horizontal wire that has barbs every 12cms. Do not use wires that have barbs placed closer as it can lead to injuries.

- **Woven wire fence:** This type of fence contains smooth steel wires that are woven with horizontal and vertical wires. This is one of the most widely used types of fencing. However, it is expensive and may not be as useful as high tensile wires.

- **High tensile wires:** You can choose either electric or non-electric fencing. It is more elastic, is lighter and more effective.

- **Interior fencing:** This may include a temporary electric fence or may use a permanent fence that divides the area. This helps cattle stay in one area without any conflict or territorial behavior.

It is a common practice to use electric wires. But make sure that your cattle are trained to recognize the electric fence before you introduce them into a pasture with this type of fencing. You can start by using one strand of hot wire at very low voltage near the water sources. Even a mild current is enough for the cattle to recognize an electric fence and make sure that they stay clear of it.

4. Transport and handling

Once you have decided the breed of miniature cattle that you want to bring home, you can look for a reliable source. The next thing that you should do is to make sure that you transport your cattle in the right way to reduce any stress that is related to travelling.

There are legal considerations when you transport cattle to make it a more humane process. According to the Code of Accepted Farm Practice for the Welfare of Cattle, here are a few things that you need to keep in mind when you are bringing your pet home:

- The transport vehicle should be of the appropriate size and design to make sure that your entire stock can be transported comfortably.

- The transport vehicle should be in good condition. That way, you will not have any injuries due to protrusions or other issues in the container. You can also ensure that the cattle will reach the destination on time without any delay due to breakdowns.

- The stock crate should be examined thoroughly. It should be smooth and the contact surface should not have any protrusions.

- In case the transport crate has any pens, they should not be more than 3 meters in length. That way the animals will have enough support during the travel and will also feel less stressed as a result of that.

If you are travelling with the following classes of miniature cattle, it is recommended that they are placed in a separate pen or crate for comfortable transport:
- Adult bulls
- Polled or dehorned cattle
- A cow and a suckling calf
- A pregnant female
- Cattle that are different is size

Here are a few things that you should do when transporting your calves:
- It is best that you hire a trailer or a transport truck for your mini cattle.

- The front of the trailer should be solid enough to protect the calf from any wind.

- The animal that is being transported should be checked on at least every 3 hours.

- You must feed the animal 6 hours before you transport him or her.

- The number of animals in the trailer should be such that they can lie down when they are being transported.

Here are some things that you must never do as it causes maximum stress:
- Never transport a mini cow or calf in the boot of your car or in a sealed container that does not allow air flow.
- The legs of the animals must never be tied to restrain them.

- The trailer should ever be overloaded. Even if it means that you may have to make multiple trips, the trailer should only have as many as it can accommodate comfortably.

These simple precautions will ensure that your miniature cow does not feel very stressed after the journey. That way, it will be easy for you to introduce the animal into your property on the first day.

5. Introducing cattle to your property

The housing area should be ready when your cattle arrives. Even if you have a temporary paddock, it will be helpful for the first day. That way, you will not have the need to tether the animal after the already stressful journey to your home.

If you have other pets or other cattle on your property, it is necessary to give your new mini a space to relax in. A paddock or a temporary enclosure will ensure that the mini is not harassed or disturbed by other animals or the general activities on your farm. With a separate enclosure, you will also have a chance to observe the animal and make sure that there are no signs of any illnesses. This will keep your family and the existing pets safe.

When your cow arrives after the trip from the breeding facility or the source that you obtained him from, here are a few things that you must look out for:

- Any wounds or injuries on the body that may have occurred during the transport.

- Uneven gait or even lameness.

It is possible that your new pet will not feed or drink much water on day one. This is normal but must diminish as the animal gets used to the new home. If feeding issues persist, you can have a vet come over and examine the animal to be sure that there is no illness.

Water and food must be made adequately available to your new pet. You can introduce the animal to hay or other food that you normally provide for the other bovines on your farm. Water is most important as it helps the animal cool off and rest well. On an average, the amount of water required is as follows:
- Dry cows or adult bull: about 70 liters each day
- Lactating cows: about 90 liters each day

- Young calves that have been removed from the mother recently: 55 liters.

You need to make sure that the water that is provided is fresh and clean to ensure good health of your new pet.

Avoiding any interaction during the first few days is highly recommended. Unless you are sure about how to approach cattle, you need to be cautious. No doubt, these miniature animals are extremely gentle and friendly. But, until they are familiar with all the sights and sounds of the area, the interaction must be limited to one person who will feed the animal and provide water.

When you notice that the cow is comfortable and is relaxed in the paddock, you can introduce your family members as well as other cattle to her.

6. Introducing your new cattle to an existing herd

If you already have a small herd or miniature cattle or regular sized cattle, proper introduction is the key to maintaining peace within the herd. What you can be sure of is that there will not be any ugly fights. They tend to establish the pecking order quite peacefully. But, with introduction of new cattle, the biggest concern is potential health risks to the existing herd.

You need to make sure that all precautions are taken before you allow your new pet to graze with the existing herd or even stay with them in the same housing area.

Precautions to avoid diseases

Even when you have the healthiest miniature cow added to the property, you must remember that the immunity of the animal will be compromised because of the transport stress, the new environment and the change in food and water. This is one of the main reasons why you need to take all the precautions possible before you introduce the animal to the existing herd.

Things to do:

- Even before you transport the new cow, you need to have a complete blood test done. Look for an authorized lab or consult your vet before you agree to buy a mini.

- The breeder should be reputable. This can be checked with the help of testimonies from other buyers. In most cases, an experienced breeder will help you with practical tips to introduce the new animal to a herd.

- If you got your mini from an auction, you have to get a complete health check up to be sure that the animal is not carrying any diseases even if he or she looks perfectly healthy.

- It is a good idea to keep a check on the exact delivery time of the cow. Have your vet on site to assess the new pet as soon as they arrive to prevent any problems at a later stage.

- It is advisable to keep your new cow quarantined in a separate enclosure for a minimum of 14 days. It is better if you can quarantine for 60 days. This will give the new animal ample time to get accustomed to the new place and will also give you a chance to observe closely for any signs of disease.

- Keep a tab on the journey time. In case there have been any problems with transportation, you must load the animal off at an authorized staging post before bringing him or her home.

- A staging post is an area where new cattle are screened and prepared to be moved into a new farm. You can find several authorized staging posts close to you online.

- Insist on vaccinations for more assurance on the health of the animal. The most important vaccines are those for bovine viral diarrhea, leptospirosis and bovine rhinotracheitis. These are the most infectious ones and can spread within the herd in a few days if you do not take proper care.

Things NOT to do:
- Never accept previous blood tests or the ones provided to you by the breeder. You must invest in a complete test yourself before the mini is delivered.

- You must not accept a delivery at short notice. You must have everything in place on your property for your new pet.

- Do not buy any cattle that is being sold in a hurry. Breeders will insist that a particular member from their stock 'must be sold today'. Even if it is a rare breed that is not readily available, a rushed or heavily discounted sale is often made for a reason, mostly a possible health issue. This is not a risk worth taking.

- Don't rush into a purchase. Plan well and investigate the breeding facility well. It is much harder to get rid of diseases in a herd than finding the perfect miniature breed for your home. If waiting can prevent diseases, make sure you do that.

Introduction to the herd

For the most part, your mini will be safe in a herd when introduced. Cattle seldom get into aggressive fights. But, if you have regular sized cows and bulls in your herd, taking precaution is necessary. The sheer size of the other animals can lead to dominant behavior.

A temporary fence can be placed between the new pet and the existing herd when you let them all out to graze. Supervise the herd during this period to see how they respond. If they are not very alert and practically ignore the newcomer, it is a good sign. You can keep them in adjacent pastures for a few days to help them get used to the smell and sight of one another. This is recommended especially if you are introducing a bull to a herd which already has a mature bull.

It is a good idea to avoid any introduction of a new bull during the mating season. This can lead to some squabble. When you let the new member interact with the herd without a fence, it should be monitored at all times initially. If there is any sign of head butting or chasing, you must isolate the new cow or bull immediately.

When you feel like the herd is getting along with the new member, allow short unsupervised introductions. Leave them together for half an hour and come back to check on them. This time period can increase slowly as they get used to each other.

It is advisable to separate polled and horned animals. If possible, you can have a separate herd of miniature cows and one with regular sized cows. That way, there is no room for dominant behavior at any point.

If you do notice any bruises or cuts, contact your vet to understand the source. This also brings us to an important point of introducing the new member to the herd on a weekday. That way, you can be sure that the vet is available in case there is any untoward incident or injury to the new animal.

4. Introducing a mini to a dog

If you have a pet dog at home, it is necessary to make the introduction correctly. With pets like cats, the risk is lower as they will not approach the cow or bull in most cases. The interactions are also limited because of the nature of cats. That said, even cats must not be left unsupervised with your cows. The size difference means that the cat is at the risk of being kicked or trampled if he startles the cow.

But, with dogs, they usually run around in the yard and will frequently interact with your new miniature cow. So, proper introductions are necessary.

The first introduction should be with your dog on a leash. Watch the dog's reaction. Frothing at the mouth, the tail pointing upwards or a hunting position means that your dog is in an attack mode. This is natural the first time they meet. If you can calm your dog down and let him watch the cows while on leash, do so. If not, try to introduce them again.

With frequent meetings, the dogs will become less responsive in an aggressive manner. It is still not safe to let the dog run freely around the cow. To begin with, the dog has a natural predatory instinct towards a cow. Second, a startled cow can cause serious damage to a dog with one single blow with his strong legs.

Allow them to interact with a temporary fence in between. Keep an eye on your dog's reaction. With regular and controlled meetings, the dog will begin to ignore the cow and lose interest in her completely.

Only a dog who is obedience trained is safe to leave with the cows without any barrier. The most important commands that your dog must respond to are stay and come. If you do not get your dog to respond every time, work on his obedience skills before he is let out with the cows.

Some cattle owners and farm owners suggest an e-collar to prevent any attacks. However, the safer way and the gentler option is to train your dog to obey commands flawlessly. This is one of the most important things for dogs that will work on farms. Once they are trained and comfortable, you can even get your dog to herd cattle for you and keep them from escaping from your farm or yard.

Special training is available for herding dogs. You can look for trainers who will help you with this and make your dog an important part of your journey with your miniature cow.

If you are lucky, the first interaction itself will be calm and easy. If not, work with your dog and help him make new friends!

31

Chapter 3: Caring for a Miniature Cow

Maintaining the health of your cattle comes from good husbandry and care. There are a few things that form the basics of proper cattle care and you need to ensure that you take care of everything to keep your heard safe and healthy.

Here are some tips to provide best possible care to your beloved miniature cattle.

1. Feeding miniature cattle

While the type of food required by mini and regular sized cattle is practically the same, the quantity is what matters. Now, a rule of thumb is that a cow or bull will consume his own body weight's equivalent over the month. So if your cow is 100lb, he will need 100lb of feed every month.

You need to make sure that your cow gets all the nutrients required for proper growth and development. It is not as simple as just placing a stack of hay in front of the cow. You need to investigate the requirements of your cattle and understand what is required to fulfill the nutritional requirements. You may have to provide different types of feed to meet the nutritional requirements of your miniature cattle.

The forage quality is of great importance. If you are unsure about the ration formulation, you can even consult a breeder or your vet to provide you with tips. The cattle needs to be assessed to understand the requirement completely.

Assessing cattle

You have to first assess the requirements of your cattle to make sure that they are getting what their body demands. Here are a few factors that you must consider:

- **The environment of the animals:** Depending on what is naturally available to these animals in their local environment, you can prepare a nutritious meal plan for them. The local environment also affects the demands and the water requirement of each
- **The productivity status of the cattle:** You can divide cattle into various classes based on the growth, lactation and reproduction as well as other categories including the gender, breed, fat level, weight and the amount of weight gain or loss required. Based on this you can formulate a ration for your miniature cattle.

- **The current climatic conditions:** The climatic changes affect the animal based on the thickness of the hide, the hair condition and the depth of the hair.

There are two options when it comes to feeding your cattle, you can either stick to dry-lot feeding where the food is harvested and stored before giving it to your cattle, or let the cattle graze if you have a large enough pasture. With dry-lot cattle, if you are unable to offer a bedding of straw or sawdust and provide mud instead, it will affect the level of consumption to a large extent. However, the nutrition requirements should be kept in mind irrespective of the kind of feed you offer.

What to feed your cattle

If you provide your cattle with only a grain mix or grain feed, the feeding technique is called feed-lotting. Essentially, cattle are anatomically designed to consume grass or roughage. Grain feeding involves providing cattle with a certain ration that consists of a mix of different grains.

For a balanced meal, it is a good idea to allow the animals to graze at least once a day and then provide them with a grain mix or hay and alfalfa grass. While nutritionally, grass feeding and grain feeding will not have too much difference, the latter makes the cattle stressed as it is far removed from their normal biological need. Therefore, a mix or adding supplements to grazing cattle is recommended.

Avoid hay as a substitute for grazing. Naturally, hay makes for less than 10% of the diet of cattle. Confined Grain feeding is usually directed towards helping the cattle grow fast. This is a practice followed in show animals as well as in animals that are mainly reared for meat.

Essentially, a grain mix consists of a mixture of Soy hull, molasses, whole oats, cracked corn, canola mean and a Vitamin B1 supplement. You can also add some calcium carbonate to this mixture to make your cattle's digestive system healthier and to prevent any bloating.

Cattle require trace minerals in small amounts. There are two types of minerals you need to provide; macro minerals and micro minerals. The former is required in higher levels than the latter. Micro minerals will improve healthy hooves, hair and skin and will also boost the immune system of your cattle. If you are only grass feeding your cattle, you can add recommended supplements to fulfill the mineral requirements. Make sure you consult your vet before giving your cattle any form of supplements.

For grass fed cattle, they will need at least half an acre per head. If this is not available, you can provide fresh alfalfa grass as a substitute.

One of the most important nutrients for any animal is water. They need water in order to digest and absorb the nutrients that you are providing with the diet. In the colder and warmer months, make sure to check that the temperature of the water remains at room temperature. You may have to shift to large water troughs if you have a natural source that gets to hot or perhaps freezes over in winters.

Now, you can feed cattle twice a day. Keep the feeding time consistent and make sure that there is a gap of 12 hours between each feed. During the summers, appetite will decrease and it will help to provide the first feed earlier in the morning. You also must make sure that the cattle are eating well. Ideally, the food that you provide should be consumed within 30 minutes, indicating a healthy eating habit.

Ideal feeding routine
Good nutrition is the key to preventing several diseases. You need to have a feeding management practice or a proper routine that will help you do the same. Most hoof related diseases, that are a major concern for cattle, are related to the feeding frequency and the size of the forages and grains. If you are transitioning your miniature cow to a new diet, as well, putting them into a routine can be one of the key factors in determining health.

If you have a dairy herd, you must give them a grain mix twice each day. If your cow is milking, you can even increase it to three or four portions as recommended by your vet. This should be followed by foraging on a pasture for at least an hour.

If you are giving your cattle only mixed ration, make sure that you check all the high moisture food thoroughly. These herds must be checked every quarter to ensure that they are getting all the nutrients that are required for them. Make sure that you keep the mix consistent and balanced. Providing grains outside the regular mix means that your cows will begin to have preferences for what they want to eat.

You can also include dietary buffers. You will have to add about 0.8% of the dry matter equivalent to the diet. These buffers will prevent any acidosis in the rumen of your cattle.

The particle size of the forage and the grain is also of great importance. If the particle sizes in your grain mix or forage are too small and the amount of fiber provided is low, they can lead to serious health issues. You need to distribute the feed and the forage particles in a way that the cows are able to digest properly.

The processing method of the grains and the moisture content in the food also chances the availability of non-fiber carbohydrates. This is a major concern when you do not provide forage with a grain mix.

If you are switching any animal from one diet to another, you need to keep the transition as gradual as possible. For example, when you are changing the diet of a calving cow, you can increase the concentrate of feed to about 0.75 percent of the body weight. Ideally, the animals that are on one type of diet should be divided into a different group with an entirely different ration.

With smaller body weight, you need to be careful with the portion that you provide your cow with. The nutrients should be balanced. In order to develop properly, cows require vitamins, trace minerals, proteins and carbohydrates. If you are unsure of how to achieve this balance, it is best that you consult your vet.

You may change the routine slightly with weather changes. Even this should be done gradually to prevent any stress to the animal. Stress always compromises the immune system and provides a gateway for several disease causing microbes.

2. Keeping the cattle clean

Sanitation is the key to good husbandry. You need to ensure that your pet is clean and well-groomed. Miniature cows tend to have an unpleasant odor when they aren't cleaned regularly.

Bathing your cow

A good bath is needed to make sure that there is no dirt or manure on your cow's body. Of course, this needs to be done carefully to prevent startling the animal, leading to unpleasant situations. A regular bath can prevent possible infections in the skin and also the chances of any parasites affecting the health of the animal.

Here are a few steps that will help you keep your cow clean in the most effortless way:

- If you do not have access to warm water to bathe your cow with, make sure that you wait for a warm day to carry this out. Cows tend to be very unpleasant when they are washed in cold conditions. They will display bad behavior all day long.

- The first thing you need to do is secure the cow using a rope or a halter that is fastened to a collar. The best option is to tie your mini to the side of a wall or the building. Using a pole to fasten the cow will lead to her walking around in circles. The rope that you choose should not be more than 1.5 feet in length. That way, your cow can eat some grass or hay when you are bathing her, but will not get too much room to move around. A shorter rope is recommended if this is the first bath you are giving your cow or if she is known to misbehave during a bath.
- The knot that you use to secure the animal should be easy to release. That way, in case of a tangle or a fall, you can release the cow safely.
- Wet the whole body of the cow starting from the legs and then working your way up to the back. Make sure that you are cautious in the beginning as the reaction of the cow to water is unpredictable. The area around the head and face should be cleaned at the end to make sure that you do not get any soap or water in the ears and eyes.
- It is common for cows to have mud or manure stuck on the hair. You will face this issue more often with long haired minis. If there are large chunks you may have to carefully cut it out without making the coat seem different.
- If you have a pressure washer, it will come in quite handy when it comes to removing dirt from the tail or the legs. The water acts like a comb to remove this dirt from the hair. Make sure that the power washer does not hurt your cow. This means that it should not be used on sensitive areas like the face, belly and the udder.
- You need to use soap on your cow to get her fully clean. Soap up one side at a time. Then you can move to the feet and the legs. The best option is baby shampoo. You can also consult your vet to provide special soap that can improve the condition of the hair and the skin. Using your hand is good enough for most areas. A hard brush is needed on the legs and the back to remove any dirt.
- The soap must be rinsed off fully. To do this, start at the backline and then move down to the legs. Make sure that you do not leave any soap on the body as the chemicals can cause skin problems.
- Don't let the cow into the housing area. Let her walk around in the sun and dry off fully. You do not want hay and other material sticking to the wet hair, making your efforts go in vain.

Be patient with the cow. If there is a lot of squirming, allow her to settle down before you wash her. If you have a large pond that you can lure her into, it is the easiest option to give her a nice and clean bath.

Hoof trimming

Lameness in cows is a very common issue. There are several factors that contribute and may be interrelated in some cases. But one of the main reasons why cows have hoof related issues is when the hoof is uneven. That leads to an unbalanced weight on the legs causing issues with the one that is carrying most of the lead.

If one hoof is being overloaded, it will become sensitive, prone to lameness and very unstable. Make sure that you check the hooves of your cow regularly and trim them for two reasons:

- In order to restore the weight balance on all four hooves equally.
- To check for any possible lesions in the hooves.

You need to examine the cow and make sure that trimming is required. If you over-trim, you can put the cow at a risk for lameness or walking issues.

There are four steps in a good claw trimming process. Make sure that every foot is approached with this technique. This will avoid over trimming. It is recommended that you seek the assistance of someone with experience before you try to do this on your own.

Step 1: Measuring tow length

- The measurement will begin at the hairline to the tip of the toe. This is called the front wall. You will measure the inside claw present on the hind feet.
- If the claw length is more than 3 inches, it should be removed. You will make a cut that is perpendicular to the sole. When you do so, the toe will have a square end.

- The inside claw on the hind feet must be trimmed first. Then proceed to the other claws to make sure that they match. This is the same process with the front legs but you will start from the outer claw.

Step 2: Maintain the thickness of the sole

- The thickness of the sole at the toe and the length of the claw are directly correlated. The thickness of the sole will be measured from the tip of the toe that you just cut. If the thickness is more than 0.25 inches, you can reduce the thickness.

- When you trim the sole, start from the front and move to the back. The horn on the hind claw should not be removed. The sole thickness should be maintained at 0.25 inches from the tip of the toe.

- The claws that are less than 3 inches should not be trimmed. You must also never trim any hoof with a sole thickness that is less than 0.25 inches.

- In most cases you will only have to trim the outside of your rear claw. That way you will be able restore balance and remove overgrowth if any.

- When you apply pressure on the sole, it should not seem flexible after trimming.

Step 3: Measure the depth of the heel

- You can measure the depth of the heel from the bottom of the sole to just below the hairline. This measurement should be taken on the outside of the claw or the heel wall juncture.

- If you see that the measurement is more than more than 1.5 inches, you should trim the horn from that heel.

- Usually, heel depth is low in cows that are housed in an area with a concrete floor.

Step4: Maintain claw and heel balance

- The surface between the inner and outer surface should be flat and capable of bearing weight after you are done with the trimming process.

- The sole will not be trimmed if you feel that it flexes when you apply pressure with your thumb or finger.

- The heel and claw balance should be checked. For this, you can use the front walls of both legs and place them on a flat surface that will go across both heels and both the toes. It should also be measured from the toe to the heel on both feet. If you can see some light from below the flat surface, it means that you have to check the trim that you have made.

You can get a special hoof trimmer in any pet store. You can also order online or but one from the vet. These trimmers are very similar to the nail file that we use in our homes to remove any excess growth.

If you feel confident, you can go through with this. However, during your first attempt, you can have someone with experience accompany you. You may even seek the assistance of your vet if you feel like it is a difficult task for you.

When trimmed improperly, the cow struggles to gain balance when walking or just standing. If you over-trim, the animal may feel a lot of pain and is also susceptible to several injuries. Make sure that you have a step by step approach that allows the animal to calm down fully before you try to trim the hoof.

3. Cleaning housing area

A clean housing area is essential for proper hygiene. If you have calves, pregnant cows or animals with a low body condition, you need to be extra cautious as they have very little immunity towards infections and illnesses.

The housing area can get dirty really fast considering that there is going to be a lot of manure and other debris that gets accumulated over time. While you can have a bedding material that is absorbent, it is necessary to change it and clean the housing area regularly.

If there are any organisms in the housing area, there is also a chance that the milk that you consume will get contaminated. Then the shelf life of milk reduces and it may even transmit diseases to the people who consume the milk.

The floor needs to be kept dry at all times to make sure that the animals do not get any foot infection or injury. Insects are also a health hazard. It disturbs the animals to begin with and also spreads diseases in the herd very fast.

How to clean the shed

You need to be willing to use water liberally to thoroughly clean a cow's housing area. You need to have the right equipment such as a wheel barrow in order to lift and dispose the bedding and the dung after it has been cleaned. The housing area needs good drainage so that you can remove liquid waste properly.

It is a good idea to remove fodder and feed that is remaining in the manger. This will reduce any chance of fly related nuisance. When you clean the entire area with water periodically, you can eliminate bacteria, algae, any chance of viral contamination or fungi. That way you can prevent most health issues that cows are prone to.

What sanitizer to use

One of the best and most potent sanitizers is sunlight. It has the ability to destroy all organisms that produce diseases. The goal of disinfecting a shed is to make it free from any microbe that causes diseases. You can sprinkle the area with the following chemical agents for best results:

- **Bleaching powder:** This compound consists of almost 39% calcium. It is one of the best and most easily available chemicals.

- **Iodophor and iodine:** You can look for commercially made iodophore. This contains 2% iodine and is very effective against germs.

- **Sodium carbonate:** If you decide to use this disinfectant, you can use a hot solution containing 4% sodium carbonate. It will wash away certain strains of bacteria and several viruses.

- **Slaked lime and quick lime:** These ingredients are used to whitewash the walls of the housing area. They prevent several microbes from breeding in the first place.

- **Phenol:** Also known as carbolic acid, this is a common household disinfectant that also works against fungus along with several strains of bacteria.

- **Insecticides:** As the name suggests, these chemicals are effective against insects such as ticks and flies that normally transmit diseases. You can use insecticides on the crevices of walls and cracks as well. You can make solution of these insecticides and use them to spray and disinfect the most common harboring areas for these insects. Using a powerful sprayer works best, although you can use a brush, sponge or a hand sprayer. The commonly used insecticides are gramazane powder, BHC, DDT, surriithion and malathion. Making a 50% concentrate solution is recommended. However, these insecticides can also be poisonous to cattle. So take care that they do not come in contact with milk, water or any food material.

The right cleaning procedure
- First, the dung should be removed from the urine channel and the floor. You can use an iron basket and a shovel to pick the dung up.

Then transfer it on to a wheel barrow. While doing this, also remove any leftovers or bedding material.

- The water trough should be emptied. A floor brush should be used to scrape the bottom and the sides.

- The water trough should then be washed with clean water. It is recommended that you white wash the water trough with the above mentioned lime solution.

- The floor of the housing area must be scrubbed clean using a broom and a brush. Then you can wash it off with water.

- There may be splashes of dung on the wall, poles, railing and other structures. This should be scrubbed and cleaned fully.

- If there are any cobwebs, remove them with a wall brush. You must remove cobwebs periodically to prevent any allergic reaction.

- Once the housing area has been washed thoroughly, you can use disinfecting agents like phenol, bleaching powder or washing soda to sprinkle the whole surface.

Precautions
To make sure that the cleaning process is safe, here are a few tips that you can use:

- The bedding material and the dung should be removed completely.

- If any dung or bedding material spills when you are carrying it out, make sure that you clean it up instantly.

- Dirty water should never be used to clean the shed.

- If there is any fodder left over, clean it before replacing it with fresh fodder. Never put fresh fodder over the left overs.

- Watch for any growth of algae in the water troughs.

- The concentration of the disinfectants should be correct to make sure that they are actually effective. You also need the right concentration to prevent any chances of poisoning or toxicities in cattle.

Before you add the new bedding material, make sure that the housing area is fully dry. During the rainy season, it is a good idea to spray any insecticide regularly. This will keep flies at bay. You may even consider whitewashing regularly to keep the mites and ticks in the walls at bay. Cleaning the housing area once every week is recommended. If not, you must at least clear out the bedding material and wash the housing area thoroughly every fifteen days. This will prevent any unpleasant odor in the area. The more frequently you clean, the easier it is each time.

Chapter 4: Bonding With Your Miniature Cow

There is no doubt that Miniature cows make great pets. They are affectionate and are also extremely friendly. You can find a great companion in your miniature cow provided you spend some time to understand their behavior and make a connection.

Miniature cows are known to be great show animals. This means that they can also be trained with ease with some commitment. This section explains the general behavior of cows and bulls to help you understand how to have more positive interactions with your pet and also stay safe when doing so.

1. Understanding behavior of your miniature cow

In case of miniature cattle, you need to be aware of all the senses that they use. There is more to cattle than just vision. This is the key to proper interaction without startling the animal.

The different senses at work

The eyes of cattle are placed on the side of the head. This gives them a combination of binocular and panoramic vision. With this, they are able to stay aware of any predator. There is a blind spot just behind them. The eye muscles of cattle are generally weaker which means that they cannot focus on any object immediately.

They can distinguish between a few colors like red, orange and yellow better than the short wavelength colors like blue and green. This helps them survive in the wild as they are able to see blood in an instant if any herd member has been attacked by a predator. They do not have great depth perception. This is the reason for one of the most common issues with mini cattle which is refusing to step over a drain gate or to cross an area with a shadow.

Sniffing the pasture is common for cows when they are grazing but it is not certain if smell is a really important sense. They have been seen to baulk at the smell of offal or blood. They also have a secondary olfactory sense of smell that helps them identify pheromones.

The ears are the most sensitive of all sense organs. It is possible to calm your mini with some soothing music. At the same time, any loud noise can cause a lot of stress. So approaching a cow when talking loudly or yelling in an excited tone can get your cow to react in a negative manner.

Cattle have something called a flight zone. This is the "comfort zone" of your cow. If the cow has been fed in a feed lot this is about 1.5 m around them and in case of cattle that is not handled too frequently, it is about 30m. When anyone unfamiliar enters this flight zone, the cattle will either move away or just let you know that you are not welcome. This is why you need to work towards the right methods of approaching your mini. Although they are extremely gentle, getting them worked up is never a good plan.

Reading cow or bull behavior

Even in some of the most well established farms, people are seldom aware of the right way to approach cattle. This results in animals that are extremely stressed and uncomfortable. It affects their productivity and in worst cases, can provoke an attack from the animal.

Reading the body language of your pet can really help you create that special bond that you dream of. For instance, if a cow is relaxed, she will stretch after standing up. If she is under any kind of stress, the common behavior includes bellowing, butting and even kicking. These behaviors are clear indicators that the immediate environment needs to be changed.

The tail is one of the best indicators of the mental state of the animal. If it hangs straight down, the cow is very relaxed and is just getting about her routine. If the tail is tucked in between the legs, it is an indication of fear, illness or cold weather. If the tail hangs away from the body, it is a sign of caution or threat. You know that your cow is in a playful mood if she is running with the tail held out. There is a slight kink as opposed to the absolutely straight tail.

Threat behavior

If you have a cow, you will have to deal less with any threat per say. The body language is almost similar to that of a bull. But, what is important to understand is that bulls are more likely to display behavior that warns you of an attack. If you are dealing with a bull in heat, especially, you must watch out for these signs.

Bulls have some common behaviors such as challenging, threatening, female seeking, nudging and territorial behavior. No matter what the cause is, a bull will provide a threat display because he is in a state of fight or flight.

When he shows a threat display, he will arch the broad side of his back to look bigger. Then, the head will be lowered and may be accompanied by rapid side to side movement. The hair on the back will stand and the eyeballs protrude when the bull is threatening you.

You must read a direct threat when the shoulders are hunched with the neck curved and the head lowered. The neck tilts towards the object that is being threatened. Then, the bull will paw his forefeet to send some mud or dirt flying back. He will also horn the ground or rub it.

If you move away when this display is on, you will probably have no further interaction. On the other hand, if you keep approaching the bull, he will end up fighting with the horns and his head.

When you see this display, it is best that you exit as fast as possible. You need to get at least 20m away from the bull if you want him to ignore you fully.

With bulls, behavior may change as per the season. For example, when a cow in heat is nearby, he will be more defensive. So, you must never expect a certain behavior even if the bull has been extremely gentle with you. Watch for signs and move away when you have to. It is best that you keep a bull with a mate or in a herd. Interacting with a lone bull is often considered harmful. You must also never turn your back to the bull. If you are milking a cow, the bulls must be restrained away from her.

The better your interactions get, the calmer your animal will be. Never tease a calf for instance. Rubbing the horn area or the head or petting the cow like you would pet a dog is never a good idea.

If you want to pet your cow or bull, stroking behind the ears or under the chin can be very comforting.

Approaching a cow or bull correctly
A method known as low stress livestock handling is the best approach to handling cattle. You need to study the animal first and then prepare the animal for your approach. There are many reasons why you will have to approach the cow or bull besides petting and playing. You have to let them out into the pasture for grazing, feed them, move them when you have to clean the housing area and lead them into a vehicle in case they need to be transported for a vet visit or any other purpose. In no scenario do you want to startle the animal and cause unruly behavior. Even a miniature cow is a lot to handle when she is in a flight mode.

Most owners make a mistake in the approach. This can sometimes lead to bad behavior all day long or may lead to an immediate negative reaction.

When you see a cute mini Hereford or Dexter, it is natural for you to make sounds that are excited. Normally people move head on and try to touch the animal. Remember the flight zone. When you continue to approach it, the animal feels threatened. This makes the animal perceive you as a threat. Naturally, they will get upset, uneasy or angry. These are emotions that they cannot handle. Cows are prey animals and anyone who approaches them displays the same behavior as a predator. A predator will just move head on and attempt to catch prey.

Even circling your cow is a predator behavior that makes them react to you negatively.

Now, imagine that you are driving on a freeway and a car is moving towards you in a straight line. The first reaction that you will have is that of fear. Now, if the car changes the line of movement and you notice that it is turning or moving around you, you become calm. The fear reaction can be intense or mild depending upon the speed of the approaching vehicle.

We calculate the angle that the car is approaching us at and decide if it will be a hit or a miss. This is exactly how your cow will react if you walk straight towards them. It is a good idea to get close enough to the animal so that we do not enter that pressure zone and then move in an oblique direction. This straight to oblique path will let the animal remain calm and comfortable. This is the same principle that you will apply even to a cow that you know well and even older cows who are extremely docile generally.

The next question is, how do you know when you are in the flight zone? It is quite simple. When you get to this zone is when the animal will take notice of you for the first time. You will see them looking at you or trying to move away. This is when you will change your angle or just stop in place. The goal is to make sure that they do not move away from you. The moment you see an alert body language is when you make the change in your path.

When you do this regularly, they learn that when they feel the pressure of you approaching them, this will be released by you on your own. They will learn that they do not have to move away in order to be safe. They know now that you will not get so close that it will bother them. When you fail to do this, the animal will feel the need to run. If there are calves in the herd, the female will feel a lot more pressure as she cannot leave her little one behind.

Read the signs exhibited by the animal and adjust your movement. When your cow becomes familiar with your presence, you can get closer each time till you can get close enough to touch her without really scaring her.

Never move towards the animal with your hand held out. This looks like you are about to attack. The other thing that you need to keep in mind is that you must never hold any object that will make you look larger. This includes sticks, a baseball bat or any other object that adds height. The bigger the approaching object, the more nervous the cow is going to get.

You will also avoid any sudden movements like waving the hand, opening your arms out to hug the animal or running. The calmer you are, the calmer your pet will be. If you have visitors or children who want to meet the cow, you have to be strict about the way they approach her. If they leave the animal in a bad mood, you will have to deal with her all day long. Worse still, if the animal gets into a flight mode, they may head butt or kick in defense. You must be extra cautious when you approach a bull.

2. Training your mini cow

While not many people think of cow, regular or miniature, as pets, the truth is that they can be a lot of fun to be around. Miniature cows are very playful and their small size also makes them more approachable.

Now that you have learnt all about approaching the cow correctly, the next step is to train them. Cows and bulls can be trained for shows and also to run errands on your farm. This training practice makes the bond between the owner and the cow a lot stronger, as it has the potential to build a lot of trust.

Halter training

This is a very important type of training if you want to present your miniature cow or bull in cattle shows. Also known as halter breaking, this process is time consuming and requires a lot of patience and persistence from your end. Irrespective of the breed that you have, it is best that you start this training when the cow is very young. The advantage is that you will be able to handle a calf better than an adult who is much stronger. Halter training a cow is very similar to a horse. Of course, the behavior of the two animals is quite different which means that you have to change your approach quite a bit.

When you are halter training cattle, the methods differ based on the age and the size of the animal. It is easier to get a calf on a halter and lead him around for a while. In case of older animals, they will take some time to get used to the halter and will also need to understand what you really expect from them.

Typically, a calf that has been weaned from the mother recently is the easiest to halter train.

The technique mentioned in this section is effective on the younger calves and the older ones. The method itself was devised for cattle that are still not of the weaning age, that is, about 6 months of age. However, it works equally well on cattle of all breeds and ages.

Catching the calf

The first step is to get hold of the calf that you want to train. Leading them into a smaller enclosure is a good idea as they will not have too much space to run away from you.

If the calf is just a few days old, they tend to be a little dopey. That means that you can lead the calf to a corner and then get hold of him. The mother should not be around, especially if she is not halter trained herself. She will show you signs of discomfort when you begin to corner the calf and try to get a lasso around the neck so that you can lead them to halter training.

When they are older than a week, it is harder to catch the calf. However, if you learn how to approach them calmly without startling them, you will be able to get a lasso around the neck quite easily. Using this lasso, you can lead the calf to the part of the farm where you wish to have the halter on him.

That said, be prepared for a lot of resistance when you try to pull a calf by the neck using a lasso. They will try to break free as quickly as possible and will put up quite the fight. Wait for the calf to settle down and take a few steps forward. Do this till he is walking comfortably with you.

Now if your calves have been bottle fed, they are most likely used to the presence of human beings. In that case, the protest will be absent and you will also find it very easy to catch the calf. All you have to do is present the bottle that you feed him from and he will walk towards you voluntarily.

Getting the halter on
When you have successfully lead the calf to the area that you want to halter him in, you can begin to do so while you keep a strong grip on the rope that you used to lead him.

The halter will go over the head and the ears first before going over the nose. The ears should be looped through the halter to make it fit comfortably. A rope halter will have an adjustable portion that will go on the nose. You will keep it as wide open as possible when you get the nose of the cattle into it. Then, you can tighten the rope around the muzzle.

You also have the option of using a leather halter that will go on the same way as a rope halter. Make sure that the head piece is snug but not so tight that it pinches the muzzle. Use a non-show halter to begin with.

If the calf has been unruly in the past or if you are dealing with an older cow, having a head gate installed is a good idea. That way, there is no chance of the calf running away when you are just half way through getting the halter on. You also will be able to prevent any injury to yourself if the calf or older cow is unhappy with the halter and reacts in a negative manner.

Following this you can connect the lead onto the metal ring that is present on a leather halter. With a rope halter, you do not have to add a lead as it already comes with a rope that is attached to the halter. Once this is done, the halter should be left on for a few days, preferably a week. That way, the calf gets used to the halter and will also understand the amount of pressure that is applied on the halter in case he accidentally steps on it. You will move on to the next step only when the calf is comfortable with the halter.

Stay close to the calf
This should be done especially if you are not bottle feeding the cow. That will help him get used to your presence. You can give him range cubes and other treats when you are around. Hand feeding is recommended as that will encourage the calf to approach you comfortably. If your calf is not particularly fond of range cubes, you can even offer some grain from your hand. The goal is to get him to approach you rather than you having to corner him or chase him around to catch him.

Keep the housing area of the calf extremely clean and make sure that he is not in a crowded area in the resting area. The lesser the stress, the better the response to halter training. You must also talk to him in a calm voice at all times.

The next step is to practice tying the calf using the halter lead. Make a few loops of the lead around a post and then tie a knot. That will keep it sturdy and will prevent the calf from breaking loose. The distance between the post and the head of the calf should not be more than 12 inches.

The first time you tie the calf, keep him there for not more than 30 minutes. As he gets used to it, you may increase the time being tied. When the calf is tied up, stroke his chin or ears to make him feel relaxed. This will also lead to positive associations with you in the future.

Using the lead

The next step from there is to actually get the calf to walk on a lead. Hold the lead in your hand and keep it short in length. Slowly walk forward and encourage the calf to do the same.

You must stay on the left side of the calf. Never allow the calf to lead. You must stay ahead. If the calf tries to step ahead of you, just stop, collect the calf and start only after he is beside you.

Never drag the calf along as you walk. Pull gently and encourage the calf to walk. When he begins to walk, just release the lead a little. You will do this till the calf learns to walk next to you. It may take several attempts. So, be patient.

Then, you can start turning when you are walking the calf on the lead. You have to watch out for any signs of protests such as jumping or pulling back. If this happens, calm down, get the calf beside you and then continue with the training. Try not to let go and keep a strong grip on the lead.

In an event that the calf escapes, catch him calmly using the methods mentioned above. Once that is done, you will continue to train. The training session will always end on your terms. If not, he will pick up bad habits like pulling. The more you practice, the better you will get at leading the cow using a halter.

Training cows to pull carts

Cows make great draft animals and have always been used to pull loads across farms. The fact that they are extremely strong makes it easy for them to pull a cart with a few farmland items on it. But, the other thing to keep in mind is that they are easily spooked by an object following them around. That is why training them gradually to get used to the cart is necessary and requires you to take one step at a time.

Unless your cow is used to being lead with a halter, she is not ready to pull a cart. When you are able to lead the cow without much protest, it will be easy to get them used to a cart.

Now, like any other training that you provide, the earlier you begin, the faster the results are going to be. It is also much easier to handle a calf. However, since you are working with miniature cows, you should be able to handle them comfortably even when they are adults.

With minis, you should avoid heavy farm work on a large piece of land. This work is typically carried out by stronger and more robust animals like oxen. With minis, you can get them to pull small weights across a short distance. Each breed has a different draft power. You can talk to your vet about this and decide how much volume of work your mini will be able to handle.

Traditionally, cattle that originate from upland areas have better pulling ability and are considered to be ideal draft animals. One of the best documents about the draft strength of each breed is available with the German Agricultural Society.

To begin with the training you can put a horse collar around the neck of the cow. Using an open collar is a good idea as the head of the cow is much larger. The horse collar will be used upside down as the head of the cow is designed opposite to that of a horse with the sensitive part around the neck.

You will notice that the trace hooks are higher on the neck. This is alright as the cow must be drawn higher. You need to add trace chains and a backband to complete the drawing gear.

If the cow seems comfortable then you can move on. If not, leave the drafting gear on for a while and just practice putting it on for a few days.

Next, you will add some sort of dead weight that the cow will have to lug around. For instance, you can tie an old car tire, a log or just about anything that is only heavy enough for the animal to feel the presence of the object. Observe how the cow reacts. She should be comfortable and calm. When she is settled down, you can try to walk her around or turn her around to get her used to the weight.

The last thing you need to check for is if the cow will pull a real cart. Use a lightweight sleigh to begin with if possible. Place a few objects on it and hook it on to the trace chains. Urge the cow to move forward. Don't rush or pull the cow. Be calm and start with a few steps before you want her to actually draw the cart. Some cows will take to this in an instant as if they have been doing it forever. Others may be hesitant at first.

Keep practicing this till the cow walks with a little push. Then it is time to check how she will react in case of distractions. You can use bright colored flags, ask a friend to walk in the opposite direction, loud noises and other triggers to see how the cow reacts. Keep your hold on the lead when you do this. Keep it relaxed until you see a reaction from the animal. If there is no reaction at all, it is the best scenario possible.

Lastly, you will vary the weights occasionally to get the cow used to pulling the cart. The actual cart can be attached once the cow is comfortable with the sledge. After this all you need to is practice every day for the cow to get used to the whole idea of being a draft animal performing regular tasks on the farm.

Milking the cow
Once your cow has given birth, she is ready to produce milk. Now, milking a cow is not as easy as pinching the udder to release the milk. You need to be as cautious as you can as this is unnatural for a cow if she has not been milked before. It can trigger some unwanted behavior that will lead to serious injuries. Here are some tips that will help you train your cow to be milked without any issues.

Start with a younger cow
When you work with a young cow who has probably finished her first breeding season, there are a few advantages to it:
- You do not have to worry about breaking any bad habits.
- The chances of any infectious diseases are very low.
- They will not need any calcium supplements.
- You can milk them just once to get the milk that you need.
- The schedule that you set is from scratch and you won't have to worry about the previous schedule set by the owner of the cow.
- The amount of milk produced is lower so you can practice with this to begin with.
- A young cow can be trained to do what you want her to do.

Why not older cows
- There are chances that the cow has some diseases that can be transmitted through the milk.
- She may be used to an electric milker. Switching to manual milking can be very uncomfortable for you and the cow.
- They may be on a schedule such as being milked twice a day that you are unable to keep up with.
- They may have problems like milk stones and milk fever that requires a lot of calcium supplementation when the cow gets older.

When you bring home an older mini for milking, you can never be sure of the issues attached to it. Even repeated vet consultations and a lot of research can lead to health problems and behavioral issues. It is always a good idea to begin with a new cow that has never been milked before.

This will give you the opportunity to check the medical records of the animal and then start from scratch.

Many people may tell you that if you are a first timer, it is a good idea to go for a cow who has experience with being milked. Of course, a young cow may fall sick and may have all the issues we have discussed. The advantage is that the incidence is much lower in case of a younger animal.

What the cow should do when you milk her
There are a few things that the cow must do in order to be prepared to be milked:
- She should come into the stall and stand still.
- She must be fully relaxed to let the milk down.
- She must not be uncomfortable around loud noises.
- She should be submissive towards you.

What she must not do:
The things that you should be weary of include:
- Kicking the claw.
- Snorting.
- Stepping on the milk bucket.
- Stomping.
- Kicking.
- Shaking her head vigorously at you.

It is very important that you never laugh off any aggressive behavior. If you have children in your house, you need to be additionally cautious to always leave her in a good mood after milking.

How to make the cow cooperate
There is a step by step approach to make sure that your cow is cooperative throughout the milking process. This takes some practice and dedication from your end. Following all these steps will give you positive results faster.

Getting the cow into a milk barn
You need to have a separate enclosure that is clean and sanitized for milking. The goal is to have the cow trot in comfortably when you open the door. This is the case most of the times except for the first two weeks of delivering a calf. Cows are known to forget when they are given a break from milking. Many owners claim that their cow that would once just enter the milking area at the scheduled time would have to be led in when there was a break of about 3-4 months.

If the cow shows any hesitation to enter the milking area, here are a few things that you can try:

- Fill a bucket with some grains and hold it under her face. She will follow you when you are holding the bucket.
- The next thing you can do is take the cow out to an open area and then put the harness on and lead her in.
- Herding the cow into the barn is a good idea. This works even better if you have a few helpers who can help you herd.
- If she has had a calf, taking the calf into the milking area will make sure that she follows you in.

This coaxing will have to continue for about a week on a daily basis. After this, the cow will fall into a routine and will follow you into the barn easily or will walk into the milking area on her own when you open the door.

You can even offer the cow some grain as soon as she enters the milking area. This will give her something to do when you are milking her and will prevent any attack or kick.

Keep the cow tethered
The lesser the movement of the cow, the easier it is to milk her. When you tether the cow, here are a few things that you need to do:
- The cow must be tethered such that her head faces a wall. Having a metal ring or a rod on the wall will help you do this easily. A ring is a better option as it will allow the head to move up and down.
- The lead that you have on the harness is the best option. Tie one end to the ring or rod, keeping the lead short.
- The cow should not be able to move her head from side to side. When the ring moves, she will be able to bend down and reach for the food. She should also not be able to move back and forth while you are milking her.
- The cow will be able to see you from the side and will have an idea about what is going on. That will help her remain calm throughout.

Watch for kicks
When a cow gets uncomfortable, she will use her back legs to kick the person who is milking her. This is not without any warning, however.

The leg will move in a circular motion when the cow is just about to kick. It will go back, circle to the side and then swing forward. Knowing this will help you prepare yourself in case a kick is about to come.

As soon as the back leg moves off the ground, you can say "No!" in a sharp and firm tone to get her to stop the kick.

There are other instances when the cow will just shift their weight from side to side. This is quite common and is not a sign of aggression. The cow is only trying to get comfortable. A shifty cow indicates that she is being bothered by something, perhaps a fly. She may also want to leave or may just be unwell.

If shifting does not stop after a brief period of time, you can check the surroundings of the cow. If you find nothing unusual, a call to the vet may help.

Always watch out for aggressive body language and stop it right in the beginning. Letting the behavior continue will lead to a cow who is pushy and bossy. That is the last thing you want when you are training a cow to be milked.

There are other signs of aggression including:
- Stomping the foot
- Glaring at you
- Shaking the head
- Growling
- Snorting
- Blowing

When you see any of these behaviors, stop the cow immediately. Putting the heel of the hand on the nose and saying Stop or No can help. Till the behavior stops, keep the heel of your hand on the nose. This will work in most cases. If it doesn't, then you can use a kick rope to keep the cow in place and to prevent any accidents when you are milking her.

Using a kick rope

There are several tools like a kick stop that you can buy online or from a farm supply store for yourself if your cow is kicking when milking. However, the easiest thing to do would be to use a rope that can be used to stop the cow from completing the kicking action.

Simply make a loop on the rope and then tie it around the hip bone of the cow. There is a rounded area near the back bone of the cow. You will see it on either side. That is the hip bone. Get to loop just in front of this hip bone and then cinch it up.

This way, the rope will be in the area between the udder and the hip bone. Tighten it to an extent that the cow is able to breathe comfortably. Then, the rope will do the job of keeping the tendons in the area constricted.

When the cow actually tries to kick, she will feel thrown out of balance. She may try a few times but will settle down eventually. You will be amazed at how simple this technique is. It has long been used on rodeo cow and works just as well when you are unable to prevent kicking when milking the cow.

If your cow is hairy, clipping the hair near the udder will prevent cinching when you use the kick rope and will also keep you from pulling the hair when milking her.

After she has been trained
Once the cow is comfortable with being milked, you will see the following signs:
- She will walk to the stand comfortably.
- She will stand and be patient till you are done.
- She will allow you to even pet her when you are milking her.
- She will not be startled by any movement that you make.

Training your cow can be tasking in the beginning. However, with any kind of training, a little bit of patience goes a long way. Training is not only a way of bonding but will also make the cow a lot easier to handle and interact with.

Chapter 5: Breeding and Reproduction in Miniature Cows

With miniature cattle, there are several breeding programs that are available. There are continuous attempts to create new breeds of miniature cattle. But, if you are a novice with miniature cows, the first thing that you need to learn is to identify sexual behavior, take care of the pregnant cow and then ensure safe calving.

1. Sexual behavior in cattle

On an average, miniature cattle live up to 15-20 years of age. They will become sexually mature when they are about 12-14 months old. Thereon, your cow will be able to have one calf every year. In case of bulls, they are sexually active until the age of 17.

When the cow goes into heat or estrus, the bull in your herd will also become excited. He will stay close to the cow and will often be seen smelling the genital area of the cow. This is a natural way of transferring pheromones. You will see other behavior such as resting the chin on the rump of the cow, snorting and pawing the ground. This behavior indicates that the bull is going to copulate with the cow in some time. The copulation itself lasts for a few seconds.

If you have a herd, there is a social ranking within it in most cases. The cows that are most dominant will display maximum mating.

You will be able to identify a cow in heat because she will get very excited. Then, there will be several attempts made by the bull to mount her. The level of excitement when the cow is in heat can either be strong, weak or medium. The difference lies in the breed of the cow, the age and just the individual personality of the animal.

If there are castrated miniature bulls in your herd, they will display sexual behavior that is similar to the intact ones. However, he will not be able to copulate because the androgens in the body are not present.

In case of the females, the endocrine balance determines the type of behavior exhibited. Now, there are several ovarian secretions that will determine the behavior. But, estrogen plays the most important role with respect to this.

There are many other factors that determine the level of sexual behavior such as the environment, genetics, the health of the animal, physiological factors and the past experiences. For instance, bulls that belong to dairy breeds tend to be sexually more active than those that belong to the beef breed. If you have new herd members, cows or bulls, they will get more sexual attention.

So if you have any bull that is not displaying proper breeding behavior, you can introduce a new member to the herd. If all the bulls are sexually healthy, introducing a new animal during the breeding season is never recommended.

If there are other cows in the herd that are on estrus at the same time, then the cows tend to be in a state of estrus for a longer time.

A bull is able to detect a cow in estrus in the pro-estrus stage. This is about 2 days before the actual estrus. This is when the bull begins to stay in her vicinity. The cow who is in estrus will urinate more frequently. This is to help the bull get a whiff of the pheromones.

The sexual receptivity remains for about 19 hours. When the cows are receptive, they may mount other cows or they may be mounted by other cows as well. When the female is being mounted, she gets into a rigid stance and the process is complete in less than a few seconds.

The gestation period of a miniature cow lasts for 285 days which is the same as the regular sized cow. During this period, proper care and nutrition is necessary. If your cow is giving birth for the first time, the term used to describe her is "heifer".

2. Caring for pregnant cow

A pregnant cow should be kept in a separate enclosure during the third trimester. Nutrition in the pregnant cow is very important to make sure that the calf develops properly. It is also essential to prevent possible diseases like Bovine Respiratory disease in the calf that is born.

On most farms, the common practice is to reduce feed costs with low cost feed. You definitely do not want to do that to your pet, especially when she is pregnant. You need to make sure that she gets the necessary amount of protein, carbohydrates, macro and micro nutrients.

According to the National Research Council, low quality hay does not provide the amount of protein that is necessary for a lactating or pregnant cow. In addition to this, when the protein level is reduced, the cow may even reduce the intake of food because of an inefficiency of digestion as the rumen microbial populations are unable to perform efficiently. When the food intake is reduced, the amount of energy that the cow gets is also reduced, leading to poor development of the fetus.

You need to understand how to check for the quality of the food and combine the feed in such a way that the nutritional requirements are fully met. In case you figure out that the food that you are providing is not able to provide the required nutrients, you can even consult your vet to figure out strategies to provide supplementation.

Testing forage

Now how do you know if the food you are giving is nutritionally adequate? The first thing you need to do is make a list of the food that you are giving your cow. Then you can have the forage tested to understand the chemical composition of the food and then determine if it is good enough for your cow.

The National Forage Testing Association is the authority in the United States. You can find the certified labs to conduct this test in your area on www.foragetesting.org. A sample of the feed can be sent to the lab for testing.

Importance of protein

It has been noticed that when a cow is provided with low quality forage, it leads to a lot of nutritional imbalance. In general, it contains less than 7% protein. If your mini belongs to a meat producing breed, the protein requirement is much higher. In case of cows, they cannot provide maximum performance if the protein in their body is inadequate while all the other nutrients are being provided.

If you figure out that the quality of fodder that you are providing is low, then you will have to give the cow a protein supplement in the later part of the pregnancy to ensure that the nutrient requirements are met.

Mineral nutrition

The metabolism of a cow can only be sustained if she is able to get enough micro and macro nutrients. They play a very important role in the formation of bones, are important components in the hormones and result in the secretion of hormones, maintenance of water balance and amino acid components. They also act as anti-oxidants.

Cows need at least 17 different minerals including Zinc, chromium, selenium, iron, manganese among others, just before calving. Although this has not been investigated thoroughly, it is suggested that the immunity of the calf can be compromised to a large extent if the pregnant cow does not have access to these minerals. This increases the incidence of diseases like Bovine Respiratory Disorder.

The forage that you supply accounts for a part of the mineral requirement of cows. If there is any deficiency, it can be managed with mineral supplements that are recommended by the vet. The level of trace minerals in the blood can be evaluated to monitor the level of deficiency in the cow before calving.

Although there is no solid evidence to suggest that nutrition and immune function of the calf are interrelated, it has been concluded that the improper secretion of antibodies and hormones in the calf can compromise the immune system.

The colostrum of "first milk" after the calf is born transfers a lot of immunoglobulins to the calf. This helps prevent diseases and keeps the calf protected for at least 24 hours after birth. If the calf is not given the colostrum, they are at a risk of developing several complications that will lead to poor body conditions and expensive treatment procedures as well.

Besides proper nutrition, you will also have to make the environment of the pregnant cow free from any stressors. This includes noises or other animals. You must provide her with a quiet corner. This is especially needed in the last trimester when the cow can start to get a little uncomfortable.

When your cow is ready to give birth, it is best that you leave her alone and let nature take its course. Sometimes, the cow may need assistance. We will discuss about how you can help deliver the calf. In case you are unsure of this, you can speak to your vet for more assistance.

3. Birthing process

The first and most important thing that you need to do when your cow approaches the time of delivery is to keep her in a secluded barn or housing area. If not, you will have to look around for her all over the property. When cows do not have a warm and quiet birthing area, they will find one themselves.

It is a challenge to look for the cow or heifer when she goes into reclusion on her own. It is also not the best thing to do to approach a cow who is trying to get some peace and quiet. With a barn where she is familiar to your movements, she will be much calmer.

Then, you will observe what stage of birthing she is in. If it is only the first stage, you will see her standing up and pacing around. They will lay down and get up several times. If you can get close enough, you will see the water sac hanging from the birth canal. It will be yellowish in color.

Usually, immediately after the appearance of this spherical sac, the feet of the calf begin emerging.

The feet should be pointing toward the ground. If not, you are having a breached birth. Observe the cow after the feet start to emerge. If she is able to push the calf out on her own, then it is best that you let her do so. If you see that after the feet have emerged, she has stayed in the same position for more than an hour, you may have to provide necessary assistance to pull the calf out.

You may or may not have to restrain her. If the cow is sitting and settled, you should be able to pull the calf out without any hassle. But, if she is standing and you are not sure if she is tame enough, you can restrain her for your safety.

Using a head gate is the best possible option. If you do not have one, you can get a 10" gate to restrain her. The head gate is recommended as it will prevent any accident or damage if the cow begins to panic and decides to back on you.

You will need a pair of shoulder gloves for hygiene purposes. Start by washing your hands from the shoulder to the fingertips. Then put the gloves on when your hands are fully dry. It is necessary to apply some lubricant on the gloves to reach in and help pull the calf out. You can try a vet recommended lubricant or can use petroleum jelly. You may have to reach into the birth canal to check on the position of the calf.

Depending on the position of the calf, you will be able to provide the right kind of assistance to the cow. Here are some positions that you can expect:

- Backward position: In this case, you do not have to turn the calf around. You will have to wait till the hind legs of the calf are presented before you provide any assistance. You will use a calving chain or any flexible rope that can be fastened to the calf in order to pull it out as quickly as possible.

- Breach position: This is when the calf is going to be born head first. This is when you have to get the calf into the correct position to avoid any complication. Push the calf into the uterus as much as possible. The flexed hock will then be pushed away from the calf. The fetlock on the foot should be pushed back inward. Hold the hock joints and the fetlock tight and bring the foot over the pelvic brim into the birth canal. This should be done for both the legs. After that you can tie the rope or the calving chain and begin to pull the calf out.

61

- Head down or head back position: The calf must be pushed back into the uterine cavity. With one hand hold the calf stable and cup the other one over the nose of the calf. If you are unable to hold on to the head, you can even hook two fingers to the corner of the mouth to get a grip. Once you have hold of the calf, you will turn him around to the normal position to make the birthing process simple.

- Foreleg back position: The calf will be pushed back in to the uterus. Then, grab the upper leg and pull the calf forward enough to allow the knee to reach forward. Tightly flex the knee and pull forward. After you have flexed the knee tightly, you will cup the hoof with the hand and then bring it to a normal position.

- Bent toe or caught elbow position: The calf should be pushed back into the uterine canal to adjust the position of the elbow and foot. If there is a caught elbow, you can grab the leg that is shoved further up and then pull it forward. As soon as you correct this, the calf will come out quite easily.

Once the calf is in the normal position that you can pull it out from, you can use a rope or a calving chain around the front leg of the calf and then pull it out. It is best that you use a double half hitch knot. You can put one loop on the fetlock and the other one just below the knee. When the cow is straining, you will pull. When the cow begins to rest, you need to stop pulling, too.

If a calf puller is available to you, make use of it. It will help you prevent pulling the calf out too quickly and causing damage. The calf puller is a U-shaped part that is used on the rear of the cow to attach the chain and pull the calf out. The puller is used at the base of the tail while the chain is attached to the legs of the calf.

As you pull the calf, you can tighten the rope or chain enough to get the calf out easily. When you feel that the tension is good enough to get the calf out, you can work in the same rhythm as the contractions of the cow. Keep increasing the tension as needed to get a better grip. At one point you will notice that the puller is no longer needed. This is usually when the calf is half way out. Then you can unhook the chain and then pull the calf out by hand.

As soon as the calf is born, the first thing that you need to do is assist it to breathe. The nose should be cleaned out using your finger to get the amniotic fluid out. Follow this with a gentle tickle in the nose using a piece of hay. You can also put a few drops of water in the ears to get the calf to shake its head. In extreme cases, you will have to provide artificial respiration to make the calf breathe. Ideally, a calf should breathe within 60 seconds of being born.

The calf should be shifted to a new pen which has clean straw as bedding. After that, you can let the mother enter the area and spend time with the little one.

The mother and the newborn calf should be allowed to rest in a quiet area. The mother will lick the calf clean and then persuade him to begin nursing. The mother cow needs a good amount of hay and clean water to relax after the strenuous birthing process. Make sure that you keep her area clear of any disturbances such as a sudden sound or even too much activity.

4. Mother and calf behavior

Just between 2-5 hours after birth, suckling behavior starts as long as the mother is standing. The calf will butt at the udder of the mother when he is learning to suckle. Heifers take more time to stand as the first birth is always difficult. Experienced cows will stand up much faster.

In order to stimulate breathing, the mother will lick the calf constantly. This simulates circulation and also excretion. It is common for the cow to hide the calf as an instinct. This is to prevent predators from attacking the helpless young calf. The cow will probably showcase this behavior even when she is on your farm.

Suckling begins with the front teat normally. It is most intense as soon as the calf stands up. The calf and the mother continue to increase the distance between them after calving. After some time, they will begin to communicate by vocalizing.

In the first week, the calf will follow the cow. If you have a herd, you will notice that the calves form a group of their own and stay in that group while the cows graze. This group is called a nursery and is an indication that the calves will begin to graze on their own soon.

You may even have a guard cow who will observe the behavior of the calves in the initial period. Cows are also ready to foster other calves when they are nursing. The number of calves that are nursed varies from one cow to the other.

When the cow is ready to give birth, she will seclude herself from the herd and will find a quiet place. If that is not possible, the herd will interfere leading to a disruption in the bond between the mother and the calf.

If you removed the calves from the mother as soon as they are weaned, you can condition them better. This will help you get them used to human handling and will also be able to take care of procedures like dehorning, castration and others. They will be quieter and easier to handle as they age. When they are constantly in human contact, they will be less stressed when they are expected to do so at a later age. If the calf is left with the mother, they may be taught to avoid human interaction as a behavior. They will pick up other behavior as well that will make them hard to handle.

The mother cow uses the vocal, visual and olfactory senses to identify the calf. When a cow begins to groom the calf, she labels the calf as her own. In most cases, the calf will stand up in just 45 minutes of being born.

The mother will aid suckling by adjusting her body in a way that is easier for the little one to access. Until 7 months from being born, the suckling time of the calf is about 34 minutes. The frequency is between 4 to 5 times a day. Studies have revealed that heifers or female calves are weaned at the age of 8 months while bulls are weaned at the age of 11 months.

The mother and the child should have a dry and soft surface to rest on. Then the calf will be cleaned by the mother. If you find that she is licking the calf for too long, it is good to separate the two so that the calf has more time to nurse and feed with the mother. The hormonal activity in the body of the mother will determine her maternal behavior.

You cannot really predict maternal behavior in cows. So, one that makes a great mother may not necessary produce a heifer who has the same maternal behavior. But, the bond between the mother and the calf is quite strong. Within just five minutes of being born, the mother and the calf will develop a specific maternal bond that helps the mother identify, nurture and protect her little one.

But sometimes, there can be abnormal maternal behaviors that you need to have checked by a vet. If left unattended, such calves may be in danger of being injured or staying malnourished as the mother refuses to feed them.

5. Abnormal breeding behavior
There are some behavior patterns in the cow that you should watch out for. If the misbehavior is targeted towards the calf, you must seek professional help. It may even help to find a foster for the newborn.

- Mismothering: This is usually noticed in cows that are in a very intensely managed maternity group. In most cases, a very difficult birth that could have been long and painful, the mother will not stand up for suckling. Even the calf may be too weak to suckle. Allowing an experienced cow to foster the calf may work. If you do not have that option, hand feeding is the next best alternative.

- Nymphomania: Yes, it is possible for your cattle to exhibit this behavior. If the cow belongs to a dairy breed, this behavior is more common. You will see that the cow begins to behave like a bull. She will begin to paw and will mount other cows or will simply not allow a bull or another cow to mount her. She may even become aggressive. Nymphomania has been associated with cysts in the follicles.

- Buller-steer syndrome: If the cow is raised in an improper feedlot set up, she will display this health problem. This behavior tends to attract many bulls who will mount the cow taking turns. This leads to serious injuries and the buller needs to be segregated from a herd. Almost 2% of the steers in a feedlot tend to display this health concern.

- Illnesses: If your cattle has any health issues, it will lead to abnormal behavior. A cow that is healthy will be alert at all times, will be vocal and will display behavior like stretching when they get up after a period of complete rest. But, an unwell cow will not move fast, will have dull eyes and will seem to be disinterested in the environment. They may also stop eating and nursing. There are several other indications of poor health including teeth grinding and hunching the back. We will discuss this in detail in the following chapter.

There are options to normalize and modify this behavior through procedures like endocrine implants. It is also easier to handle cattle that have been neutered or spayed. If you are not interested in breeding your miniature cow, you can get them neutered at a young age to avoid these behaviors.

Normally, sexual behavior that is not ordinary is the result of endocrine imbalances, genetic issues and also poor management. The good news is that you can reverse most of this behavior with help from proper professionals.

It will also help to learn more about breeding behavior and general cattle behavior to make the environment less stressful for your cow. Nutrition plays a big role in leading to good behavior. For instance, a bull who is on a high protein diet will show more urge to masturbate.

In the breeding season, especially, the surge of hormones may lead to difficulty in handling your miniature cow. But with some patience and knowledge, you should be able to manage most situations effectively.

6. Raising calves

Taking care of a newborn calf is no piece of cake. You will require a lot of patience to make sure that the calf is comfortable and is developing properly. There are several reasons why you may have to take on this role. The mother may succumb to a difficult birthing process, she may develop abnormal behavior or you may just prefer to have a calf that is hand raised. It is best that you handle the calf after it has been weaned. But, if you have to take care of a newborn calf, here are a few tips and techniques.

Rearing a newborn calf

If a newborn calf has been orphaned, you will notice depression, dehydration and a loss of appetite. You will have to provide proper care for the first 24 hours to make sure that the calf is healthy and to ensure survival.

Colostrum is needed for the newborn calf in order to be healthy. This is the first milk that is produced by the mother. Passive immunity against possible health threats is provided with the colostrum which is rich in minerals and vitamins.

In the first 36 hours of being born, it is necessary for the calf to get this colostrum. You can either get it from the mother or can opt for artificial sources. If you have several cows in your herd that are calving, it is advised that you take one portion of the colostrum and freeze it. You can look for milk replacers that contain colostrum as well.

As soon as the calf has consumed the colostrum, he can be given whole milk or a milk replacer. If you have frozen colostrum, you can hand feed the baby. It should be warmed to 36 degrees before you feed it to the calf. In case you have a good supply of colostrum available, you can feed it to the calf for the first two days. You must give him two feeds, one in the morning and one in the evening. Each portion should consist of at least 2 liters of colostrum for it to have the desired effect on the development of the calf.

If the calf is born dehydrated, you will have to rehydrate it before feeding. A calf that is dehydrated will have scours or may not even survive if he is given milk before rehydration. You can make an electrolyte mixture at home or can purchase one from the vet.

At home, electrolytes can be made by adding ½ teaspoon of baking soda, 1 teaspoon of table salt and 125g of glucose to about 1.2litres of water. Before you give the calf any milk, make sure that he has received the electrolyte for at least 24 hours to rehydrate completely.

Feeding options

Cattle have four stomachs and are called ruminants. When the calf is born, only the fourth stomach or the abomasum is the one that is functioning. It is harder to feed a calf with teats but when the calf suckles, the esophageal groove responds by closing and directing the milk directly to the fourth stomach where it is easily digested. Using teats will also stimulate the production of saliva and will urge the calf to take in more fluids. The teats should be kept clean at all times and if there is any deterioration in the condition of the teat, it must be replaced.

You have the option of using a bucket to feed the calf as well. But the issue with the bucket is that the esophageal reflex is never triggered and the milk will go straight to the rumen. The rumen is not functioning at this point and the milk stays undigested. This leads to scouring or diarrhea in the calves.

When you use a bucket, you need to make sure that it is at least 30cms above the ground. This will help the groove close and prevent the milk from entering the rumen. If your calf does not take to the bucket instantly, you will have to train him to do so. Straddle the neck with the calf backed into a corner. Moisten your fingers with milk and take it to the mouth of the calf.

No matter what method you use, the calf should be given a measured amount of milk. When the calf gets older, he will begin to graze. Then, the other stomachs will begin to develop. So, you need to make sure that your calf has a good amount of high quality hay in order to stimulate the proper development of the rumen.

Controlling illnesses

One of the most common issues in young calves is scouring or diarrhea. This can lead to death very quickly if not treated properly. When you notice this in a calf, make sure that he is taken off milk for a minimum of four hours during which he is provided with a good amount of electrolytes.

In case scouring continues after this, you will need proper medication to help the calf. This should be provided only after consulting the vet. When you are expecting a calf, keeping this scouring medicine handy can save the newborn's life. Make sure that the sick calf is isolated.

You must always keep the environment of the calf hygienic. If you are using teats, make sure that it is cleaned properly and is maintained in good condition. This is one of the best ways to prevent any illness in hand raised calves.

The calf must always have ample water to drink. This will keep them healthy. Calves will not drink any water up to two weeks of age. By the time they are six weeks old, they will be consuming almost five liters of water each day. You cannot expect water to be replaced with milk even if you are feeding the calf twice a day.

The water bowl needs to be cleaned regularly as the calf may foul it while feeding. You must also allow the calf to interact with older ones that have a fully developed rumen. This will help them pick up some necessary microbes that aid digestion of food in the rumen. They are passed on from one calf to the other when they graze on the same pasture. They can also be spread through behavior like licking which is very common when calves are being introduced to one another, almost like an approval.

How to make a calf feeding program successful
- If you are using milk replacers, make sure that they contain 10% fat, 20% protein and not more than 10% of starch and sugar. Reconstitute the feed and provide it as per the instructions given by the manufacturer.

- You can increase the portion of the powder if you are feeding the calves only once in order to reduce the volume of food required.

- If you are feeding more than one calf, you will draft them as per the feeding habit.

- Milk should be divided into separate feeds. One can be given in the morning and the other in the evening at a regular time. As the calf grows and begins to forage, you can give him one feed a day. Make sure that he has a lot of cool and fresh water to drink at this stage.

- Good hygiene is a must when you are hand-raising a calf.

- You must never over fed a calf. This is especially important in the first three weeks of their life as it may lead to diarrhea or scouring. You must feed a calf 10% of his body weight every day. For example, if the calf weighs about 20 kilos you will provide 2 L of milk every day.

- The milk should be at a temperature between 35 to 38 degrees.

- Clean water should be provided at all times. The water trough should be cleaned out regularly to prevent the chance of any diseases.

- You must never alter the amount of feed that you are giving the calf suddenly.

- As calves get older, they will need more food. Milk replacer is an expensive option. It is a better idea to make up for the required volume of food with grain and pellet. You can make this available at all times. They will feed on their own and will slowly increase the amount of grain that they consume. This will make it a lot easier for you to wean the calf when the time comes.

- When you switch to solid foods, make sure that good quality hay is introduced along with concentrates when the calf is about two weeks old.

Weaning a calf
- You can wean a calf more easily at a younger age. Providing milk up to 12 weeks of age is good enough as long as the calf is in good health and is developing properly.

- If you introduce grains and solid food when the calf is about one week old, you will be able to wean him off milk completely by the time he is five weeks old.

- You must wean the calf as per the consumption of concentrate. When the calf is consuming at least 650g of mean in a day should you feed wean them. Do not use age as a basis to wean the calf. In some cases, the calf will be able to reach this target earlier.

- You can reduce the milk concentration over a week to make weaning quicker and more abrupt.

- You will have to provide the weaned calf with good management. Otherwise, poor nutrition and poor management will lead to stunted growth that cannot be reversed.

- In case of young calves, the diet should contain at least 20% of crude proteins.

- Make sure you provide fresh feed every day and clean out any leftovers from the trough every time you feed.

Providing solid food
- When the calf is about one week old, you can start by providing access to clean hay all day. This will improve the activity of the rumen. By the time the calf is about 12 weeks old, the rumen should be functioning normally.

- You will only give them high quality baby calf meal or good quality pellet till they are about five weeks old.

- Green grass in excess should be avoided till the calf is 6 weeks old to prevent any indigestion.

- You can provide concentrates to the cow by adding a little to the milking bucket. Just when the calf is about to finish drinking the milk, you can rub some concentrate on the muzzle. This will encourage them to taste it.

- By the time the calf is three weeks old, you can give him meals hay, grain and access to green pasture in small amounts. Any change that you make in the feed should be gradual.

- As per the quality of the pasture, you may have to provide the calf with concentrates and supplementary hay until the calf reaches the desired body weight.

- The concentrate that you provide to your calf should have a coarse texture, should be highly palatable and should provide the calf with proteins, roughage and a lot of energy. A good mix includes four parts of crushed grain and one part of linseed, peanut, cottonseed meal or copra. You can also add a small amount of molasses to it to make the calf relish it more.

- You can add rumen modifiers as advised by the vet. This will improve the activity of the rumen and will also prevent any chances of coccidiosis in calves. You can add this as per the instructions by the manufacturer. It can be added to pellets, molasses based food mix and also pre-mixed meals. You must not add it to any urea based supplement.

- Rumen modifiers should be provided in small quantities as an excess can be toxic.

- You can provide protein meals as a natural source of bypass and rumen degradable proteins.

- You must never provide non-protein sources of nitrogen such as urea when the calf is very young.

- The best hay for young calf is Lucerne hay. It should be checked for any weed or mold before feeding it to the calves.

- In case you have a pasture that is scarce or is not of good quality, supplementing the feed with good quality hay will work wonders.

As discussed, rearing and hand raising calves can be a difficult task. The goal must always be healthy development of your pet and if you have any queries, you can speak to your vet for more suggestions.

Chapter 6: Miniature Cow Health

Maintaining your miniature cow includes proper care and food. Above all, you need to make sure that your cow is free from any illnesses. If you are rearing the cow for milk, you need to be extra cautious as there are several bovine diseases that can also be transmitted to humans through milk or through the environment.

From finding a reliable vet to having a proper program to prevent common illnesses, this chapter will take you through all the aspects of perfect healthcare that you need to provide to your mini.

1. Identifying illness in miniature cows

Providing timely assistance is key to maintaining your miniature cattle. Only when you are able to identify a possible illness will you be able to provide the right medication at the right time. Be observant of your mini and make sure that you note down any deviation from normalcy. Here are some definite signs that your cattle will display when sick or injured.

Check the body temperature

If you keep a regular tab on the temperature of the cow's body, you will be able to identify an illness almost immediately. In several calves, the best indication of illness is body temperature as they provide very little or confusing visual signs.

The thumb rule is that any increase in temperature above 104 degree Fahrenheit in rectal temperature is a sign of illness. Of course, you must never neglect visual signs irrespective of the body temperature of the cow.

The body responds in the most natural manner to disease causing organisms. The immune system prepares to fight the infection, thus causing a temperature surge. In some cases, the cow will be able to overcome the infection on their own and will recover without any signs. In other cases, you will have a noticeable increase in body temperature along with other visual signs. Neglecting this will lead to worsening of clinical signs and may lead to death if the cow is not treated.

The earlier you detect an elevation in body temperature, the more effective the treatment is.

The biggest problem that you will face with cattle is that there is no "normal" body temperature per say. The body temperature is minimum in the morning and continues to raise through the day. This heat load is shed fast as night time approaches, enough to reach a minimum temperature in the morning. This fluctuation of body temperature occurs even in the colder months.

During day light hours, the temperature will increase even when the temperature of the environment is controlled and maintained at a standard. So it is clear that not only the environment affects the body temperature of cows. There are several factors like the level of activity, feeding, humidity and solar radiation that affect the body temperature of cows. You will see rapid increase in body temperature after the cow has eaten or after any exercise.

This is the primary reason why cattle must be allowed ample rest after sundown. While it may seem like a good time to take them out to the field, they have to rest in order to let go of the body heat. This is especially true when the day is very hot.

On warm days, it is critical to note the body temperature of the cow in the afternoon. Many farm owners will allow the cattle to rest or just stand for about three hours before they measure the body temperature in the afternoons.

You must also follow this procedure to minimize any form of stress before you take the body temperature.

Visual signs of illness
Suppression of appetite is the first give away of illness in cows. When a cow is exposed to any respiratory disease, her appetite will begin to decrease in just 48 hours from infection. This is long before an elevation in body temperature is noticed.

Make sure that you observe your cattle whenever you feed them. You cannot really monitor them when they are grazing on a daily basis. However, you can monitor them by checking the gut fill of the cow. If the belly is bouncing as she walks and the cow looks gaunt, it is a sign that she may not be eating as well. She may have also stopped consuming water in the required quantity. If the body condition deteriorates and the weight reduces rapidly, it is an indication of illness.

There are other signs that you need to watch out for including:

- Deep coughing
- Depression
- Drooping head and ears
- Slow movement

- Lagging behind when in a herd
- Reluctance to stand up
- Nasal discharge
- Eye discharge
- Bloody diarrhea

These symptoms are noticed after the animal has stopped feeding properly and after the rectal temperature is high. So, the more you observe your cattle, the faster you will be able to get them the treatment that they need in order to fight an infection.

Sometimes, these signs of illnesses can even be caused by a vaccination provided to the cow. When you put your cow on any vaccination program, be sure to check with the vet about the possible symptoms that you can expect. That way you will be able to distinguish if the cow is actually ill or whether she is experiencing a temporary side effect caused by the vaccination.

Cattle manure can also be examined to determine whether your cow is sick or not. If the manure is loose and has large particles of feed along with blood and mucus, it can indicate some sort of injury. In case of a grazing herd, you cannot really separate the specific cow or bull. Then, an abnormality in the manure is a sign for you to become alert and keep an eye on the herd. It is common for a cow to defecate when being handled. Make sure that you keep an eye out for any abnormality when you are doing so.

Identifying injuries
The injuries in cattle can range from minor to severe. Sometimes, it is easy to detect the injury upon observation. These injuries usually manifest in the form of lameness or inability to stand up. With such injuries, it becomes hard to sell a cow. Besides that, you do not have to worry about the general behavior of your pet after she has been treated.

There are other injuries that have more subtle signs and symptoms. These include bruises and any form of organ damage that can be caused with diseases like hardware disease. You can expect such an injury if the animal shows sudden changes in appetite and becomes reluctant to move.

You must examine the immediate environment of the cow to make sure that there aren't any potential hazards that could have led to an injury. The horns of other animals in the herd can also cause a significant amount of bruising. This is most common during breeding season or if you are not providing enough food leading to competition within the herd. If there are any sharp objects such as nails in the handling area and the pastures, they may injure the cow as well.

The key to treating injuries is to observe the animal when you are feeding them or washing them. You can check for any mild laceration or cut, blood vessel ruptures, mouth injuries, foot injuries, eye injuries or any damage caused by insect bites. In order to notice these injuries, you will have to make sure that you pay close attention whenever you are handling the animal.

In most cases, this can be treated in your home while keeping the cow restrained. If you are unsure of the type of injury and the treatment, you may have to contact your vet immediately to check the cow.

When you notice that your pet is sick or injured, it should be managed immediately. It is very common for cattle to be put down, on large farms, because the initial symptoms were ignored. You certainly do not want that for your beloved pet mini.

Work with your vet to figure out a program or a routine that can keep the health of your mini in top shape. If there are any situations that are not included in the plan, you can contact your vet for any assistance. The more you learn about cattle health, the better you will be able to prevent diseases and illnesses in your pet.

2. Common health issues

There are a few diseases that your miniature cow is prone to. If you have raised a regular sized stock, the diseases that affect them will affect a miniature cow as well. Here are some diseases that you much look out for:

Tick borne diseases

Tick damage:
- The damage caused by ticks is mostly around the ear and udder area. These wounds tend to get infected and will eventually be attacked by flies.

- Certain ticks like the ones that cause heartwater infection tend to cause more damage in cattle than other types of ticks.

- Treating for ticks is necessary every week during the rainy season and every fortnight during the dry season.

- If the cow is vaccinated, then you will be able to treat them less often and still prevent tick borne diseases.

- Ticks will infect cattle with several diseases like gall sickness.

- European breeds tend to be at a greater risk of getting these diseases.

- The older the animal, the greater the risk of tick borne diseases.

- Vaccination and other preventive measures can be taken against tick borne diseases.

- It is best that you have the calf vaccinated before the age of 6 months to make sure that they stay free from tick borne diseases.

Redwater
- Redwater is accompanied by symptoms like
  - Red urine
  - Pale and yellow gums
  - Pale eyes
  - Loss of appetite
  - Nervous signs such as inability to walk.

- The cow may succumb to this condition if not treated appropriately and in time.

- Keeping the cattle free from any stress is a big part of the treatment program. Make sure that you do not graze them over long distances.

- It is advised to inject them with Imizol or Berenil.

Gall sickness
- Gall sickness can be passed on by ticks and can also be spread when one animal comes in contact with the blood of an infected animal through insect bites, using same injections for all your cows or dehorning.

- The symptoms of gall sickness are:
  - Depression
  - Lack of appetite
  - Pale to yellow gums

- Constipation
- Fever

- The animal tends to be ill for a much longer period in case of gall sickness in comparison to heartwater or redwater.

- The cattle should be allowed to rest as a part of the treatment program.

- You can provide the sick animal with doses of tetracycline or Imizol.

Heartwater
- The most common signs are:
  - Depression
  - Fever
  - High stepping
  - Convulsions

- When left untreated, death is inevitable with your miniature cow if she is infected with heartwater.

- The best possible treatment is tetracycline.

With tick borne diseases, proper hygiene and timely care is the best way to prevent any complication. You must also control the insects in the housing area to prevent diseases from spreading from the infected animal to the others. It is a good idea to isolate any cow who has severe tick infestation.

Diseases that can be transmitted to humans
Cattle health is extremely important because it can influence your well-being as well. Here are a few diseases that can be transmitted from cows to human beings.

Brucellosis

- This is a disease that will affect the fetus in a pregnant cow. It is highly infectious to people.

- The disease is transmitted to people when they consume milk that is untreated when the animal has the disease.

- In people, this condition will lead to symptoms like night sweats, muscle pain and loss of appetite.

- The condition can be prevented with a vaccine after testing the blood of the animal.

- The female calves should be vaccinated between the ages of 4-6 months.

- It is a good idea to have the state vet or the animal health technician in your area check the blood samples of the cow for brucellosis.

- Normally, a cow that is tested positive for this condition is branded with the letter C. Make sure that you do not buy a cow with this brand.

- There are several diseases that can cause abortion in pregnant cows. This condition is the most important of them all as it can be dangerous to humans.

Tuberculosis
- Sudden weight loss is the most sure shot indication of tuberculosis in cattle.

- People can get this condition when they drink the infected milk.

- A simple skin test can be done every year by the state vet to check if your cow has tuberculosis.

- When an animal is tested positive for tuberculosis, he will be given a T-brand on the neck.

Cattle measles
- This is a type of measles that is caused by tapeworm in cattle. It can infect people only when the meat of an infected animal is consumed.

- Usually cattle will pick up tapeworm eggs when they are grazing. The cause for infestation of the pasture is due to poor toilet practices by people in some areas.

- The measles are not visible in the animal and is normally seen only when the meat is cut.

- Proper hygiene is necessary to keep the animals free from tapeworm infection.

Anthrax
- This disease can lead to sudden death in cattle.

- People catch the infection when they consume the meat and also through cuts and sores on the animal's body.

- If an animal has succumbed to this disease, it is best to bury or burn the carcass.

- The only way to prevent the condition is with proper vaccination.

- In case you have any suspicion of an anthrax infection, you may want to check with your state vet.

Rabies
- This is not a very common condition in cattle but an infection can be caused if the cow is bitten by a rabid dog or jackal.

- The cattle will either be too excited and aggressive or will seem like he has no energy at all.

- If you reach into the cow's mouth for a routine dental examination or if you are bitten by a cow with rabies, you can be infected.

- It is only possible to vaccinate a cow against rabies as there is no cure once the animal has been infected.

Food related issues
Sometimes your miniature cow may ingest something untoward when grazing. Monitoring the pasture is a great way to prevent these issues. However, if you see you any of the following symptoms, contact your vet immediately.

Eating wires or plastic bags
- When cattle do not get enough food, they may voluntarily eat these items. It is also consumed when you do not include enough potassium in the diet of your cow.

- Buying bales of hay with a wire around them can lead to ingestion of the wire.

- Even when the cow gets close to a new fence or one that has been fixed recently, it can lead to wire ingestion.

- Plastic bags are extremely harmful as they block the stomach. On the other hand, wires tend to puncture the stomach. In either case, the animal will seem uncomfortable and sick. If not attended to, the animal will die.

- A surgical process is the only option when the cow has eaten any wire or plastic.

- You can prevent this by ensuring that your cow is on a good diet.

- You must also keep the area clear of any plastic bag or wire.

- Cattle must be observed when they are grazing.

Poisonous plants
- When your cow eats any toxic plant, she will be seriously ill. In some cases, the plant can prove to be fatal.

- You must be aware of the toxic plants in your vicinity. You can speak to your state vet for any assistance in this regard.

- If you bring in new cows to your home, they are at a greater risk of poisoning as they are not aware of the plants that could potentially be toxic.

- You can also expect possible ingestion of poisonous plants when you introduce your cow to a new paddock.

- One plant that is extremely poisonous is gifblaar. It is most common for this plant to cause poisoning in the dry season. During this season, this seems to be the only plant that is green and can easily attract the cow.

Foot related problems
The hoof is one of the most sensitive areas in your cow's body. It is the area that comes in contact with moisture and dirt and when not maintained well, can get seriously infected. Some of the most common foot related issues are:

Laminitis

When the dermal layers of the feet have an aseptic inflammation. This leads to sensitivity and inflammation. The symptoms of the condition are:

- Moving in a stiff and cramped manner.

- Standing on the toes while moving to the very edge of the stall is a common way to reduce pain.

- Hemorrhages in the sole.

- Yellow coloration of the sole.

- A white line may appear in the junction between the sole and the wall of the hoof.

- Cracked heels

- Double soles

Sometimes the animal may not show any sign of lameness or pain. While you cannot point out to one causal factor, some of the most significant reasons include:

- Increased fermented carbohydrates leading to acidosis of the rumen.

- Poor nutritional management.

- Hormonal changes during parturition or the lactation cycle.

- Digestive or metabolic disorders.

- Infections such as foot rot, meritis and mastitis.

- Hard surfaces in the housing area.

- Lack of proper bedding.

- Overstraining of the body.

- Undesirable walking surface.

Rumen acidosis
- This is one of the primary contributing factors to lamintis.

- It is caused by the ingestion of more carbohydrates than the rumen can ferment.

- Fiber digestion is reduced and the production of lactic acid increases.

- When the amount of fermentable carbohydrates in the food increases, the amount of rumen bacteria also goes up, producing a lot of fatty acids.

- Eventually, the pH of the rumen reduces affecting the bacterial population negatively, leading them to diminish.

- When pH is below 5, the amount of lactic acid produced increases. This leads to acidosis.

- This, in turn triggers the release of several endotoxins that leads to histamine release.

- Eventually, the lamina is destroyed, hoof deteriorates and laminitis occurs.

- Histamine is normally released when the cow is stressed. So it is possible that even environmental stress and an infection may lead to rumen acidosis.

Acute laminitis
- Systemic illness is noticed in case of acute laminitis.

- The corium is very evidently inflamed.

- The condition may recur if the metabolism rate is not restored.

- Swelling and an increase in body temperature is the first sign of acute laminitis.

- You will also notice a coronary band in the area that consists of the soft tissue.

-

Subclinical laminitis

- Inflammation leads to hemorrhaging eventually.

- The horn tissue grows and the hemorrhage moves quickly to the surface.

- The sole is normally 0.4 inches thick. As the hemorrhage rises, the thickness increases by 0.2 inches each month.

- This is why the hemorrhage is only noticed about two months after the infection.

- If you notice these sole hemorrhages and any yellow coloration of the hoof, the condition could be rampant in the herd.

Chronic laminitis

- You will see a lot of changes in the area of the digit where infection occurs.

- The keratinized horn changes shape and begins to look more broadened, flattened and elongated.

- There is a rippled appearance on the surface of the claw.

- You will notice a dish like formation on the sole and in front of the hoof wall.

- The coffin bone is separated from the front wall of the hoof internally.

- You will see double soles with a yellowish tinge which indicates a major clinical problem.

- When the condition becomes more severe, the coffin bone will begin to protrude from the hard tissue on the sole.

- When the disease begins to manifest in this way, it is not possible to treat and bring the foot back to normal.

- The frequency and intensity of each case of acute dermatitis episode determines the extent of damage caused.

Digital dermatitis

- You will notice foot warts that look like yellow and red patches in the area above the heel.

- These warts can be very painful and will also bleed from time to time.

- As the lesions mature, they can become larger and go up to 2 inches across. They also have growth of tufts of long grey or brown hair like projections.

- This way the wart appears to be hairy.

- These lesions will persist for several months and will usually reduce as the dry season approaches.

- It is suspected that the condition is caused by spirochete bacteria.

- It is very contagious but is responsive to medication 90% of the time.

- Poorly drained stalls and wet stalls lead to this infection.

- You will find this bacteria in the digits of healthy cows as well but there may be no infection.

- Several cases have been reported when the infected animal shows no signs of illness or disease.

Other bovine diseases

There are several other diseases that affect cows particularly. Here are a few that you will have to watch out for in order to keep your pet safe from any chance of infection.

Bovine Respiratory diseases

- Also known as shipping fever, this is a type of pneumonia that is caused when the calves have been shipped.

- There are several other factors that can lead to this condition.

- Stress related to dehorning, weaning, weather changes and shipping will make the cow susceptible to these infections.

- It is natural for the cow to feel some stress when they are made to travel. However, this can be managed by handling them carefully and keeping the conditions within the shipping vehicle sanitary.

- Vaccination is the best preventive measure against this condition.

- Make sure that the calf is vaccinated when he is very young. If not, they will not be able to survive should they contract this disease.

Backleg disease
- The medical term for this condition is clostridial disease.

- While there are over 60 strains of clostridial bacteria, not all of them will cause the condition in cows.

- This condition is more common in cows that are younger than 2 years of age. A gangrene formed in the muscle is the main reason for this infection.

- When the young calf does not get ample colostrum, this disease may occur.

- In older cattle, it is the result of the contamination of the vaccination needle.

Bovine respiratory syncytial virus
- This condition can be fatal in cattle at times.

- It is normally caused due to stress and may lead to severe diseases of the respiratory system.

- It will also compromise the immunity of the animal against several other diseases.

- The common symptoms include runny nose, high fever and a runny nose.

Bovine Viral Diarrhea
- This is one of the most expensive diseases contracted by cattle.

- The common signs are nasal discharge, fever, coughing and scurs.

- The more severe form of this disease is known as Type 2 Bovine Viral Diarrhea.

- It leads to hemorrhaging in young calves and can also lead to severe infections in the adults.

Infectious Bovine Rhinotracheitis
- This is a mild respiratory disease that often compromises the immunity of the animal.

- It is dangerous as it opens up the possibility of several other infections and diseases.

- The virus is shed through discharge in the eyes and the nose.

- In non-vaccinated animals, infections can be caused through the nasal passage and the mouth.

Haemophilus Somnus
- This is a type of bacterial infection that can lead to a series of neurological, reproductive and respiratory diseases in the cow.

- The common signs are rapid breathing, inflammation of the nasal passage, deep cough and a loss of appetite.

Pasteurella Multocida and Pasteurella Haemolytica
- These are very infectious diseases and can cause pneumonia in the cow.

- These bacteria tend to multiply very rapidly when there is any stress, poor husbandry, primary infections and poor weather conditions.

- The symptoms include:
    - High fever
    - Loss of appetite
    - Lethargy
    - Depression
    - Sudden death.

- If the animal does survive, he usually has poor body condition because of the lung damage caused by this condition.

Tetanus
- This infection can occur when the animal gets infected because of the wounds or when improper castration and dehorning procedures are carried out.

- The body of the infected animal will become stiff leading to death eventually.

- In the early stages, the animal may respond to penicillin treatment.

- It is best that you prevent the condition with appropriate vaccination.

Lumpy skin disease
- This is yet another important disease that is geographical in nature. When certain insects bite the animal, it leads to this condition.

- Normally, lumps are observed on the skin. If the lump enters the body of the animal, it may lead to death.

- The best way to prevent the condition is to get the cow on a good vaccination program.

- Should your mini get infected, consult a state vet immediately.

Three day stiff sickness
- This is another condition that is caused by insect bites.

- It will lead to lameness in the infected animal and in some cases the animal will just lay down and stay there.

- The symptoms last for three days after which they disappear on their own.

- You will have to take food and water to the animal if he is unable to stand up.

- The condition can be prevented with a proper breeding program.

Pink eye
- The clinical name for this condition is Bovine keratoconjunctivitis.

- It is very common among large herds and breeds like the Hereford are predisposed to the condition particularly.

- The infection is caused by a type of bacteria called *Moxella bovis*.

- The disease is treatable. However, it will affect the production of milk to a large extent.

- In the warmer months when the dust increases, the flies hover in larger numbers and pasture stubbles occur, your pet is more likely to catch the infection.

- When you see a lesion in the center of the eye, it is a sign that the infection has begun.

- Eventually, the eye will turn red and tear production will increase. As the infection gets more severe, it can lead to the development of an ulcer.

- Preventing the condition from spreading is possible when you isolate any infected animal.

- When detected in the early stages, injected medicines can cure the disease. The most effective antibiotic is tetracycline.

- You also have specific vaccinations that can prevent pink eye in your miniature cow.

The best thing about cows is that they can heal wonderfully when you provide them with the right type of care and medical attention. The best way to control any infection in your pet and within your herd, if you have one, is to practice good husbandry and provide the animal with a stress free environment.

3. Finding the right vet

When you bring a miniature cow home, the first thing that you need to do is look for a vet. Do not wait until there is an emergency to look for one. The thing with cattle is that the vet should be specialized to deal with farm animals. There are fewer specialized vets who are already working with a large base of farms. So, looking for one near you and one who is conveniently accessible is a challenge.

Besides finding a vet, it is good for you to build a good rapport with your vet before you actually bring your mini home.

If your vet is familiar with your property and farm area, he will be able to make better recommendations to get your miniature cow into an effective healthcare regimen. They will also be able to come over in case of any emergency after your pet has been transported from the breeder to your home.

In areas where there aren't too many farms, it is harder to find a livestock vet. With the vets that are available, it is possible that they are already taking care of a large part of the livestock in that area. So, the earlier you build a rapport, the easier it will be to seek assistance when it is really needed.

Even if the vet is unable to visit the animal, he will be able to give you necessary advice on the phone in case of an emergency. Of course, the better the relationship, the more you can count on getting the right assistance even if it is in the middle of the night.

There are a few reliable sources that you can choose to get recommendations for a local livestock vet. To begin with you can check with the Cooperative Extension office in your area where you normally purchase food and other supplies for your pet.

They can recommend specialized vets and also one who will be willing to visit your farm when needed. You can call the Cooperative extension office and ask them for the current list of veterinarians.

Alternatively, you can even check the website of the USDA or its counterpart in other countries for a list of the closest extension office so that you can get all the information that you need on livestock vets.

There are several other experts who can help you with healthcare for your beloved pet. For instance, in a cooperative office, you should be able to find nutrition specialists. They can also give you some technical assistance when needed.

The other reliable source to get leads into local livestock vets is another farm owner. It does not matter if they own a mini or not. They will definitely be able to get you in touch with a vet who takes care of their livestock. This may include goats, chicken or any other farm animal or bird. Word of mouth is, in fact, the most reliable source.

You can also look for information on the websites of veterinary associations such as:

- The American Association of Small Ruminant Practitioners
- The American Association of Bovine Practitioners
- The American Association of Swine Veterinarians
- American College of Veterinary Surgeons
- American College of Veterinary Internal Medicine

If you live near a state university or college that has a veterinary division, you can also check with them for leads. In some cases they may have a hospital and clinic in house that will work perfectly in case of an emergency. Some specialists will also make farm visits when necessary, provided you are within a limited distance from the clinic.

When you are looking for a vet, there are some characteristics that will make you "click" with your vet:
- The vet follows the same ideals that you do when it comes to raising your mini.

- Of course, you have to be flexible in your values. There are some factors that cannot change. For instance if you prefer to grass feed your mini, your vet must also be in favor of it.

- However, there may be times when you and your vet may not have the same logic or ideals. That is alright, as long as they are respectful of your principles and are willing to work around it.

- When it comes to the welfare of your pet, you must also be willing to accept some advice from the vet even if it is not exactly what you believe in. For example, in some cases, you may have to switch to grain feed for an antibiotic to work better.

- In these cases, you can ask your vet why a certain method is better than the other. This will give you extra knowledge about your mini as well.

Once you have found a vet who is conveniently located and is comfortable to work with, you can ask the following questions to be entirely sure of the choice you make:
- What are your working hours?

- What equipment and cattle diagnostic resources are available with you?

- Are you available for emergencies?

- In case of an emergency, if the vet is not available, who will cover for them?

- What are the payment options?

- What is the regular fee per visit?

- Is there an additional charge to make a farm visit? If so, what are the charges?

- How can one contact the vet in case of an emergency?

There are several tips that you can take from your vet to provide first aid in case of an emergency. However, when the condition is serious, you should be able to call your vet who has all the skills to restore the health of your cow.

4. Preventive care

With the severity of infection in miniature cows and the rapid onset of the condition, there is no option but to take all the preventive measures possible to ensure that your pet is safe and in perfect health.

The first step is to make sure that disease resistance is high in your mini. This can be taken care of good nutrition and plenty of fresh and clean water. Cattle rely extensively on the pasture that they graze on for food as well as shelter. You will have to constantly keep a check on the quality and the quantity of grass available in your pasture.

The more important thing is to make sure that you keep the grazing area free from any debris. Sadly, people tend to throw food wrappers, drink cans and bottles out in open areas without a second thought. If any of this garbage blows into the pasture, your cow may end up eating it. As discussed, the blockage is only surgically manageable.

It is a good idea to walk the line of the fence everyday to check for loose wires, any debris and also to check the safety of the fence that you have put up.

Vaccination is a must against all major diseases such as anthrax. You can contact your vet for a list of vaccines that are recommended for your miniature. You can also contact the cooperative extension in your area to find out what vaccination is necessary for any localized illness.

The vaccination schedule must be accurate and you need to ensure that you always get the boosters in time. Worming is also recommended to prevent several health issues in your cow.

You can obtain a computerized system that will help you maintain records and track your herd health on a schedule. You can check the weight and even figures like the sale price of a certain member of your herd. When you want to change the composition of a herd or want to include a new member, these programs will give you a lot of data.

You must also invest in proper handling material such as harnesses and also proper transport to ensure that there is no hassle when you have to make a routine visit to the vet or when your vet comes over for a checkup.

There are two aspects of preventive care: Pasture management and herd management. Here are some tips that will help you take care of each one correctly.

Pasture management
- Plant the area with nutritious varieties of grass on a regular basis. This will keep the grazing composition balanced. You can mix rye, white clover, fescue, orchard grass and other types of forage grass.

- You must be able to identify all the poisonous plants in your area to make sure that they do not grow in the area. A proper program should be created to eradicate any toxic plant.

- Pasture rotation is a good idea if you have the room. When you move your herd to a new pasture, the old one should be allowed to rest for a few months.

- Picking up manure from the pasture will prevent any form of re-infection in the herd.

- If you have large bales of hay, you may want to keep them in a round feeder so that they do not rot when the rainy season arrives.

- If you notice any swampy areas or low lying areas that can accumulate mud and water, it must be fixed immediately. In case the pasture gets wet completely, you must move your cattle to dry land to ensure that they do not stand around in mud.

- The area around any natural source of water must be checked for excessive mud deposits.

- The edges of the water trough should be free from mud deposits. This will, again, force cattle to stand in mud, leading to weakening of the hooves.

- Your cattle should be offered mineral blocks, especially when they are young. For any supplementation, consult your vet first.

- Make sure that there is enough access to fresh and clean water so that they can drink to their heart's fill.

- In case you buy any hay for feeding in the winter months, it should be of the best quality possible. It must be stored correctly. Any hay that seems wet or moldy must be discarded immediately.

Herd management
- New cattle should only be purchased when you are able to find an auction house or local farm that is reputable.

- Make sure that the cow that you buy looks healthy. You must also insist on getting the health history that includes details like worming history and vaccinations.

- When you transport the animal, find the shortest routes possible. This is one of the biggest stressors for your mini.

- When you have a new cow in your home, isolate her from the rest of the herd if you have one.

- Animals that are sick and weak should not be bred.

- If your animal is sick or injured, make sure that you call the vet promptly.

The better the husbandry practices that you follow, the more will it benefit your cow. Observing the behavior of your pet can also come very handy in preventing the escalation of a condition and ensuring that timely aid is provided.

5. First aid
There are a lot of simple measures that you can take to provide immediate care in case of injuries and emergencies. Knowing how you can care for

your miniature cow is the first step to being a good owner. In some cases, it may be too late before the vet arrives or you take your cow to the vet.

Injuries in case of animals never take place in a location or time that is convenient. If you are able to take care of the injury immediately with appropriate care, you can reduce the impact of any injury.

There are a few simple principles that you can apply in each scenario with your pet. Being prepared is to have all the knowledge that is needed along with the right first aid kit. Make sure you consult your vet and learn more skills to take care of your pet.

When the animal is injured, the behavior will be very different from normal. They may not be as calm and docile as you expect them to be, so be careful when you handle an injured animal.

The first thing that you need to do is restrain the animal using a harness. When your cow is restrained properly, it will prevent further injuries to the animal and will also keep you safe.

Here are some of the common issues that you must watch out for:

Cuts, puncture wounds and scrapes
- Wash the wound with a gentle cleanser, running water or saline solution.

- If there is any debris or dirt in the wound, use a lot of saline to flush it out of the wound.

- It helps to use a large syringe or bore needle to wash the area so that you can clean the specific area.

- Even the eyewash that you use with contacts can be used to wash wounds. You can get a large container of this if needed.

- Cover the wound with some water soluble ointments and also antiseptics.

- With water soluble ointments, you will have faster results in comparison to sprays that will make the tissue dry.

- On superficial wounds, you can use an ointment that is petroleum jelly based. These ointments are not recommended when they have a certain chemical composition.

Eye injuries

- If there is any foreign object lodged in the eye it can be washed out with saline that is maintained at body temperature.

- In case you are unable to restrain a cow with eye injuries, your vet may have to tranquilize her before you do anything.

- The eyes are extremely delicate and you must make sure that you do not treat the injury unless you have adequate experience.

- In case of head and eye injuries, you and the animal can be injured severely without necessary precautions.

Bleeding
- Any form of bleeding can be controlled if you can hold the area down with gauze sponges.

- Make sure that the gauze is kept in place while you bandage it snugly enough to clot the blood but not so tight that it would restrict blood flow.

- If you are unable to control blood flow with this technique, you must call your vet immediately. This may require surgical correction.

- You can use blood stopper powder only on superficial wounds. However, these products should ever be used on deep wounds.

- If deep wounds are not treated properly, there can be tissue damage, scarring or formation of abscesses.

Hoof care
- The hood of your cow will present several special challenges.

- Any wound in the hoof must be flushed out immediately.

- For most hoof injuries, it is best to just wash the hoof and house the animal in a dry environment.

- An absorbent wrap can be used to cover the wound. Many farms use disposable diapers as effective covers for these wounds. If not you can even use cotton.

- If you are using an elastic wrap, make sure that it is not too tight, restricting the flow of blood.

Bloating and frothy bloat
- This is common in ruminants.

- It is usually caused when the forage consists of an excessive amount of succulent legumes.

- You can use commercial products like BloatGuard to break the froth down. Vegetable oil can be used in a small quantity as a reliable home remedy.

- If the animal has free gas bloat, a speculum with a garden hose is normally used.

- In extreme cases, the vet will use a bloat trochar.

Handy first aid kit for your cow
Having the right tools and equipment in place can be a life saver in case of an emergency. When you have a miniature cow in your home, you can make a first aid kit on your own with the following items:
- Heavy duty scissors
- Flashlight
- Needle nosed plier
- Halter and rope
- Wire cutters
- Disposable gloves
- Skin cleanser
- Gauze sponges
- Sterile saline solution
- Water soluble ointment
- Frothy bloat equipment
- Medical tape or duct tape
- Fly repellant
- Large syringes
- Antibiotic eye ointment
- Thermometer
- Rolled cotton
- Calcium gel or calcium borogluconate
- Mineral oil

- A small dose of epinephrine
- Hoof nippers
- A knife
- A small container
- Water based lubricant
- Phone numbers of your vet, state vet and any emergency facility

It is recommended that you have your cow checked by your vet on a regular basis. It is true that medical expenses for your cow can be high. That is an important factor to keep in mind. You can also speak with insurance companies to help you find a plan that can cover your cow in case of any major procedure.

Chapter 7: Cost of Owning a Miniature Cow

Even if you have the time and the necessary space to keep a miniature cow as a pet, you need to consider the costs involved in raising one. These costs will have to be covered through the lifespan of the cow which is about 50 years on an average.

- Cost of the cow: $1000-1200 or £500-750 on an average
- Cost of hay per month: $140 or £70
- Building the barn: $1200 or £800 on an average
- Cost of supplements: $150 or £70 per month
- Vet visit- $45-70 or £20-30 each visit

Besides this, there are additional costs such as a possible surgery in case of illness or injury, breeding costs, construction of separate confinement areas when needed and lots more. On an average, you should be willing to spend at least $300-400 per month on a family cow.

The advantage with having a cow is that you can get a good amount of returns with the manure and also the milk. You will save a lot on milk products if you have a family cow. Of course, if you plan to breed and sell miniature cows, it can turn into a profitable business.

Conclusion

Thank you for choosing this book. It is a sincere effort to make all potential owners aware of the requirements of a miniature cow so that they can manage them properly.

Needless to say, miniature cows and bulls make wonderful pets. You can enjoy your journey with them even more if you can prevent episodes of illness or bad behavior. The goal of this book is to make you equipped with enough information to do so.

For most part, miniature cows are nothing but delightful. The more time you invest in your pet, the higher are the returns. They can make wonderful companions and will literally keep you company through generations.

When you are ready for a mini cow, you can be sure that you will love every moment of having one at home. Hopefully, this book makes your journey a lot smoother and easier.

References

You can never have too much information about the well-being of your beloved miniature cow. In order to upgrade your knowledge and information on a regular basis, you can look up several sources on the internet. Here are some reliable websites that allow you to participate in discussions and also read up as much as you need about miniature cows.

www.homesteadingtoday.com

www.miniaturehereford.org

www.cattleforum.com

www.southernstates.com

www.extension.psu.edu

www.arrowquip.com

www.producer.com

www.futurebeef.com.au

www.animalbehaviour.net

www.coolcows.com.au

www.minicattle.com/

www.abcsheds.net.au

www.dairycloud.co.ke

www.apahd.gov.in

www.grit.com

www.thefarmbarbie.com

www.zugrinder.de

www.surechamp.com

www.miniaturecattle.com.au

www.backyardherds.com

www.dextercattle.proboards.com

www.hobbyfarms.com

www.farmstyle.com.au

www.sufficientself.com

www.tractorsupply.com

www.rurallivingtoday.com

www4.ncsu.edu

www.cattletoday.com